Robin Ross

1990

Loopy

Loopy

AN AUTOBIOGRAPHY

George Kennard

with a Foreword by
General Sir John Hackett

LEO COOPER

First published in Great Britain in 1990 by
LEO COOPER
190 Shaftesbury Avenue, London WC2H 8JL
an imprint of Pen & Sword Books Ltd
47 Church Street, Barnsley, South Yorkshire.

Second impression 1990

ISBN 0 85052 175 0
Cataloguing in Publication data
is available from the British Library

Printed in Great Britain by
St Edmundsbury Press Ltd, Bury St Edmunds, Suffolk
and bound by Hunter & Foulis Ltd, Edinburgh

To Nic and Zandra

and to the future generations of
Officers and Soldiers of the Regiment,
in the knowledge that they will
retain the gallantry, the loyalty
and the talent for hard work
and fun of their predecessors,
this book is dedicated.

Contents

Acknowledgements

I would like to thank my Editor, Tom Hartman, for his constant good humour, patience and hard work. Also my soldier friend, Robin Rhoderick Jones who unearthed my illiterate two-finger-typed reminiscences and with great diligence converted them into an acceptable form.

My thanks, too, to Colonel Charlton and Major Romney for their poems on amalgamation.

Foreword

by General Sir John Hackett

If anyone were to say that this is rather a mixed-up book the answer might well be that Loopy is rather a mixed-up person. First of all he is probably more widely known and better loved than any other regular British officer of his generation. I do not say 'Officer in the British Army' for a very good reason. Loopy is the living embodiment of the concept that the British Army in a very important respect can hardly really be said to exist at all, except, that is, as the structural framework which contains and supports the corps and regiments which compose it. When an officer is commissioned into the armed service of the sovereign in her land forces the commission is into a specific corps or regiment, not into 'the army', and a move into some other component is possible with a change of designation, duties and badge but again with no mention of an army. There is also something called the General List, in which some are enrolled who actually are commissioned into the army, but these tend to be few in number and special in nature. Loopy is the quintessential regimental officer, the summit of whose ambition is command of his own regiment.

The regimental system is more highly developed in Britain than anywhere else in the world and is something of which we can be hugely proud. There are many who enjoy its public manifestations, the ceremonies, the bands, the uniforms, the display of customary insignia, the emphasis on differences (a wolfhound on parade for the Irish Guards, a little pony for the Paras, a goat for the Royal Welsh Fusiliers) without realizing the importance of the system itself. There are some (among them not a few who have risen to high rank in the service) whom all this makes rather impatient. They want uniformity, units all dressed alike numbered 1-2-3, with none of this costly exhibitionism. These are people to whom tidiness is more important than common sense. They have not realized that the splendid performance of British arms on the battlefields of the world is almost wholly the product of the regimental system. Turn it over to ethnologists whose business is the study of the behaviour of groups under stress and you would almost certainly be told that the regimental system is not a quaint survival in a military museum but a military tool of deadly effectiveness. This is worth saying as the advance of military technology tends to lessen the importance of group action by men-at-arms in battle, and true dyed-in-the-wool regimental cavalry officers like Loopy tend almost to become an endangered species. Perhaps we should catch a few up while there are still some in the wild, and preserve them. Perhaps all we need do, to speak in current jargon, is to preserve their eco-system, their habitat, the regimental system itself. Then there will always be Loopies, if only very rarely another specimen so spendid.

He and I have known each other a long time, though I knew nothing of him and his family in the earlier years, of which he writes so enchantingly in this book. We both did all the riding school and training in obsolete weapons required in those days of horsed cavalry and then went to our intended regiments, he to the 4th Queen's Own Hussars, I to that of my great-grandfather (the rather incompetent Captain John Hackett of his day in the 8th Light Dragoons, now Hussars of course), through supplementary reserve service in one of the greatest of British regiments, the Queen's Bays. We did not meet even there. I was at Oxford. Loopy was due for Cambridge but his parents said they could not afford it. He took a job and then the King's shilling. Our two regiments had, however, long been close. They had ridden together in the Charge of the Light Brigade at Balaclava, one of the most extravagant displays of eccentric gallantry that even British Cavalry have put on. In accordance with a widely spread practice in our regiments of turning disaster into a festival, this one has long been celebrated with high hilarity.

In the Western Desert in World War II the 4th had had severe casualties, and had lost a good few (including Loopy, now a captive) in Greece. The 8th had been reduced to one squadron. The two remnants were put together in a welcome union which was called the 4th/8th Hussars, into which, as an 8th Hussar Squadron leader (the only one left) I was posted as second-in-command of the 4th Hussars, an honour I shall always treasure. Thus both regiments shared the battle honour of Alam el Halfa and, when made up to strength, parted and went their separate ways. But not for ever. After the War amalgamation was in the air. Both regiments were in Germany in the fifties, in that greatest of divisions, 7th Armoured, the Desert Rats, of which, *mirabile dictu*, I was myself then G.O.C.! We had to amalgamate and it was deeply planned. A splendid Indian cavalier, George Butler, had come to the 8th. I had him posted to the 4th, so that when amalgamation came about the first C.O. of the new regiment should come in badged 4H. There was much done behind the scenes, including insistence that a new badge should be devised for the amalgamated regiment (the Queen's Royal Irish Hussars) *before* the event.

It all worked and there has never been a happier marriage than the Queen's Royal Irish Hussars. Before that, however, as G.O.C. 7th Armoured Division I had seen much of 4H and learnt to admire the combination of efficiency and urbanity they deployed. This was all due to Loopy, then in command as C.O. of the 4th Hussars and the best regimental commander, in his own unique style, so delightfully dwelt on in his book, that you could find. That was all he ever wanted, command of his regiment, and he did it wonderfully well, with a panache all his own.

So here is Loopy's book, telling of the early shimmer through an exotic childhood into elegance and splendour as a dazzling but always modest young man, deprived by ill fortune of vast wealth (inheriting from a father who dispersed millions no more than a couple of frayed old Etonian ties) but turning out to be a baronet nonetheless.

I loved this book, even though I recognize at least one story I rather think I told him myself, and am greatly honoured to be allowed to write in it. The seven years I spent as Colonel of the Regiment of the Q.R.I.H. was greatly enlivened by having Loopy around as the best known of any commanding officer of a cavalry regiment and the best liked. Every year, now the 16th, as we go salmon fishing together on the Spey I rejoice in my friendship with a brave, courteous, steadfast man, emergent from a background as puzzling as any peacock's egg, about which this book will tell you much, and who represents more clearly than anyone of my acquaintance what was known, long ago, as chivalry.

Read this book and if you do not know him already you too can make this unique person's acquaintance.

Prelude

Blackbirds, which are normally happy to be around this small Devon house, have taken flight. Some, I think, are drunk – from the raisin residue of my homebrew thrown on the horses' midden.

It is a weekend and the young will outnumber the beds. The late-comers will sleep in the barn piled high with faded brocades and tables too large to fit into the house. Fortunately they all have jobs and will return to London on Monday. They are articulate and fun.

The loud cacophony issuing forth from the wireless of an arriving car will soon be replaced by a different sort of noise. Peter, now having given up hurling himself off suspension bridges from Clifton to San Francisco attached to life only by a rubber bungie, is arousing the curiosity of the cows as he assembles a small aircraft brought down on the roof of an equally small Citröen. This hideous machine will soon demoralize the wheeling buzzards, and the cows will be as frightened as the blackbirds. Milk production will, of course, fall.

Off stage, my wife is shovelling the first of many urgent loads into the washing machine. It will continue its churning until the last guest has gone.

I escape to the relative peace of my study and the charm of the letters of my great-grandparents, written in an altogether different age – an age of elegance, cosiness and not a little guile.

ONE

The Years of Elegance

Eilen Roc
Antibes 30 March 1883

My dear Kennard,

My wife and I are much pleased to know that you so entirely approve of your son's proposal to my daughter. I believe that if blessed with health, there will be in their union a prospect of happiness for themselves and their parents which falls to the lot of few.

I am willing to make an allowance to my daughter of £3000 tax-free a year, the same as you propose to give your son, and when her mother and I have gone she should have not less than £300,000, and probably a great deal more.

In the meantime, however, and to provide against all possible eventualities, I wish that we would settle a certain sum on her as is normal in such cases. I would propose, therefore, to make over securities which I now hold to the extent of £50,000; you doing the same.

If you approve of what I have written I am quite willing that the young couple should consider themselves engaged.

Yours most sincerely,
James Wyllie.

Kennard did so approve, but his son Hugh wrote of his concern as to what would happen to the Wyllie money should his future bride die childless. At least he had the grace to add that he was a 'devilish lucky fellow to get such a girl's love'. I much prefer the girl's letter to her future father-in-law:

Eilen Roc
Antibes 7 April 1883

My dear Mr Kennard,

I do not know how to find words to thank you for the letter I received this morning, but I very deeply feel and appreciate the great kindness with which you tell me that you will accept me as a daughter and can only say how much I hope in the days to come to try and repay it by doing everything in my power to be a good and loving one to you.

The future seems so bright, almost too good to be true! For I love Hughie with all my heart and long for the time when I can devote my life to making his a happy one, and pray and trust that I may succeed.

Believe me, every yours very affectionately

Helen Wyllie.

Alas poor Helen's prayers were largely unheeded for it seems that soon after the birth of my father, Coleridge, the couple indulged in endless squabbles over trivialities. Hugh, by then a subaltern in the Coldstream Guards, went on a long voyage to get away from it all. In this he succeeded – probably beyond his wildest dreams – by dying at sea at the age of 23.

She, gentle woman, repaired to the sun-filled solace of the villa Eilen Roc, there to bring up my father among its marble pillars, gold plate and woods created by planting every tree in tubs set in holes drilled into the rock.

In 1896 she married James Lawrence Carew, Irish Nationalist MP for Kildare, again to be quickly widowed, and finally retired to a suite in Claridge's where she became prey to parasites whom she maintained at the expense of a disappointing son. There she lived, was badly loved and died. She had retained the life-long affection of Oscar Wilde who inscribed her copy of *The Happy Prince* with the words 'To the Happy Princess from the Unhappy Prince, with the devotion of the Author, Oscar Wilde'. She, for her part, commissioned Epstein to execute the sculpture on Wilde's tomb in Paris.

The loss of their only son, my grandfather Hugh, was a dreadful blow to the Kennards. Ellen, his mother, Victorian and virtuous, went into heavy black from which she emerged only when news reached her that her husband was to be given a Baronetcy. Exactly for what this honour was to be bestowed I have never been clear. He had, it is true, been the Conservative Member of Parliament for Salisbury, but his only achievement seems to have been to promote a Bill allowing policemen to vote. He did, however, own the *Evening News* which he ran at a staggering loss whilst supporting Lord Salisbury in a number of windmill tilts, including that of a 'determination to deprecate a quixotic policy with respect to Egypt'.

The editor of the *News* was Frank Harris, a nasty little man who financed his round of 'all the best houses in England – once' by drawing a substantial salary from my great-grandfather. In his *Life and Loves,* Harris writes that 'I found Coleridge Kennard a funny little person who seemed very anxious to keep the paper strictly Conservative . . . he had a daughter Merrie who was both kind and affectionate and very pretty.' (Merrie managed to resist Harris's advances and married General Lord Rawlinson.) 'Kennard told me,' continues Harris, 'that he wanted a Baronetcy for his wife's sake and that he had spent £70,000 to get it, though he was told that £40,000 would suffice!' Frank Harris appears to have been an impossible hypocrite for whilst he was writing the above for public consumption, he was dedicating one of his less sex-sodden books to 'Kennard, in token of deepest respect and gratitude, from his friend the Author', and adding the self-damning couplet:

> Now, as of old, men by themselves are priced,
> For silver Judas sold himself, not Christ.

The powers that were had no sooner decided to award Coleridge his assiduously sought Baronetcy when the intended recipient died. Back into black went Ellen but her inflexibility of purpose remained. She fought long and hard and Queen Victoria capitulated to permit the 'Style, Place and Procedure' of a Baronet's widow to be bestowed upon her, to pass to her grandson (my father) on her death. A splendid coat-of-arms went with the title and the faintly fatalistic motto 'At Spes Non Fracta.'

Ellen, still in black but triumphant, died soon afterwards and I have a once-vast portrait of her by Wells; she looks quite lovely, although I had to cut her legs off to get her into this house. She seems to have been as gay, kind and virtuous as she was determined and lovely; her scrap and recipe books survive as testaments to her character.

Ellen's unremitting efforts helped to assure the comfort into which the infant Sir Coleridge Arthur Fitzroy Kennard was born. Titled at the age of six, most of his boyhood days were spent at Eilen Roc which he was soon to inherit together with many miles of seafront from Juin-les Pins to Antibes.

Through the splendid salons of the villa passed the fancy of the age. Royalty to be sure, and political figures too, Salisbury and Gladstone. Teams of gardeners raked the gravel; there was rich food in grand abundance, rocks to fish from and the glorious, endless sunshine. But only a gardener's daughter to play with.

As he grew up via Eton and the Foreign Office, he made his friends in England: Duff Cooper, Beardsley, Lord Alfred Douglas, Ronald Firbank and Harold Nicolson. It was Nicolson in *Some People* who described this brightest of new lights in the social firmament as '*d'une élégance, mais d'une élégance*'. In short the young and eligible Sir Coleridge became a great dandy – a Grand Seigneur. The seigneurial rights were exercised freely, breach of promise cases followed each other with careless rapidity. The one unforgiveable sin was to appear a bore and yet, and yet. His title, his money, his brilliant friends could not quite disguise the fact that beneath the foppish exterior an uncertain artistic temperament struggled, not always in vain. It flickered occasionally into a few beautifully written, slim and elegant volumes. The critics were increasingly delighted when the young Sir Coleridge was 'once more tempted into print'. The books were not, of course, commercial; authors who sold books for money were close to if not beyond the pale. Somerset Maugham, who later lived nearby in France, was 'that hack who wrote for money'.

> Once again I wonder why anyone chooses writing as a profession or a pastime; it is a trap that ensnares; often it positively hurts. And when all is said, what results from it? It brings no riches – those who make fortunes only dictate . . . It does not ennoble, it does not improve one's charater; nor make one more companionable. Rather the reverse.
>
> I remember I was once playing golf at Cagnes on the Riviera with Michael Arlen and Somerset Maugham. We were teeing up beside the 17th green when a metallic sound of tapping came through the wistaria from a neighbouring villa.

> 'Phillips Oppenheim hard at it,' Arlen remarked. Maugham did not seem to hear, so intent was he on listening. Suddenly his grim face grew darker: 'Michael, that's not one typewriter; it's two. He is dictating to two secretaries at once!' They both missed their drives.

You see my point? Dictating not writing.

Early in his Foreign Office career, my father was posted to Bucharest where Sir George Barclay was Ambassador. The Barclays appear in the Domesday Book and there are dozens of them still, looking after Norfolk and banks. Sir George, by entering the Diplomatic Service, had done well, at least compared with his brother who was eaten by a lion. He was completely incapable of telling a lie which so confused the foreign Courts to whom he was accredited that they recognized in him a cunning he did not possess. His addiction to the truth led him in later years to confess to his wife that he could never be satisfied with only one woman; she decamped and in her late forties married a Swiss Brigadier General. Sir George retired to solaces denied to him in marriage and, being a very ordinary poker player died in a two-roomed flat.

His lady was an American, Eleanor Jay Chapman, who had all the explosive energy and stubborness of her pioneering forebears, one of whom – her grandfather – had signed the Declaration of Independence. In her career as an Ambassador's wife she had set about bullying the Serbian and Rumanian Courts with a will, and at the same time bemusing the Corps Diplomatique by smoking cigars happily between mouthfuls of soup at grand dinner parties. She was known universally as The Lovely Lady Barclay and would probably have bolted even if her husband had not always spoken the truth. As it was she married her Swiss who was a functionary of the League of Nations and they both died when the League collapsed.

Sir George and his Lovely Lady had a daughter and it was in Bucharest that my father imagined himself in love with her. He courted my mother with such persistence and indiscretion that the Ambassador, whilst fully appreciating Sir Coleridge's elegant hand, concise reports and impeccable dress sense, sent him packing. Fatal of course; elopement was followed by marriage, and then came my brother Lawrence and me. It was after Lawrence that the marital rot set in; there were frequent quarrels, and after one particularly notable disturbance my father went away for three months travel. Absence clearly made his heart grow fonder and by means of copious cables he set the stage for a romantic reunion. It was not to be; he arrived home to be informed by his butler that Lady Kennard was out playing bridge and would not be returning until 10 pm. In spite of that there must have been occasional reconciliations because, three years later, I was conceived. But before I was born my father had bolted. Whither he went I know not or what or who took him there, but he ended up in Persia soaked in Arabian mythology, songs and silks, having found his love in mirages evoked by dope – hashish and opium. He could, if he had so wished, charmed the very Venus but now chose to live his life devoted to drugs and the more fashionable casinos. It is quite clear that he enjoyed losing heavily with a well-bred bon mot much more than he could bear the vulgarity of winning. There must have been a whole dictionary of bon mots – Eilen Roc for instance, went overnight. But he remained *d'une élégance, mais d'une élégance* and turned out until the end, courtly lines of Persian verse exquisitely bound.

Despite losing the villa, and more, my father remained in the South of France continuing to hold an eight at the same time as successive members of Greek syndicates held a nine. But then he met the beautiful Mary Graham Orr Lewis and this time he fell headlong in love.

She won him from both dope and gambling and he built her a home, the Villa Mary Graham, on a piece of the remaining coast left to him. There they prepared to be happy together; but soon after this beautiful little house was complete they bathed from the rocks below and she scratched herself on a jagged edge. In a few hours lock-jaw had put her winsome beauty into a grave together with the nicest of his heart. Five months later, in November, 1931, he wrote a heart-broken letter to her:

> All I ask is so little: the thought, the half thought if needs be, that you know how much I am missing you and longing for you.
>
> The future? To end in darkness without even finding you there to take my hand. It is unthinkable. Yes: I cannot think it because it is probably the truth.
>
> To hear the key in the door; to see you walk in – in your black astrakhan coat – and come up to me; your cheek, oh so chilly from outside, put forward to be kissed – it seems the most natural thing in the world – and yet nothing, nothing, NOTHING can ever make it happen again.
>
> Darling I write these notes to try and ease my heart-ache, but all I really want to write, all I have to say, is just this, and this alone: I loved you more than I ever knew I could love anyone: from 7 pm, July 6 1931 everything for me ended; there can never be anything for me in this life again.
>
> Just to think back, endlessly to think back and delude myself that you are not – oh God – that you are not really dead. My darling, I

> stretch out my arms towards you. If only I
> could feel that you know how I miss you.

Back came the drugs and the gambling – and a dope nurse. She was a simple soul who taught her patient simple things. But she lived a far from simple life, following the Fashion from Paris to Deauville to Tangier and back, and she never effected a cure. The war did that.

When the Germans over-ran France the British Government kindly sent a boat to evacuate the residents of the South. Sir Coleridge dragged himself away from his aperitif to look at the boat, found that there was no private bathroom for him and elected to stay. He was not alone but the British Consul had gone and, as Grand Seigneur, the others looked to my father for guidance. They also looked to him for more material needs and he was able to raise money for them by guaranteeing their loans. Most were not honoured, either at the close of hostilities or, for that matter, since. With little else to occupy him, he continued his philanthropic work until the Germans arrived, whereupon he moved into a hotel at Aix so stupendously expensive that the only other occupant was a very rich Jew. This singular state of affairs attracted the attention of the local Gestapo who removed both occupants to concentration camps, my father being transported to Compiègne. They questioned him closely on the elegant Persian transcripts kept in his old Foreign Office red box, convinced that they were coded reports. He asked the Germans to allow his nurse to accompany him and since they would allow such a move only if they were married, he gave us a new step-mother. The transition from caviar to potato peelings and from champagne to ersatz coffee resurrected in Sir Coleridge the best in him that Mary Graham had briefly found and nurtured. He survived to quip at victory, much respected by the other inmates; he had, at last, found himself a man and died, perhaps luckily, before he was able to resume his old ways.

Alas, he forgot to make a will: by French law his property went to his widow who, honest woman that she was, fully intended to leave it to Lawrence and me when the time came. Time, however, beat her to it and within a few weeks she, too, was dead and the lot went to her sister who nearly expired from the shock.

Now the only connection I have with that expensive coast is the main street of Antibes, still called the Avenue James Wyllie – and the Statue. The Statue was erected to Wyllie by the town and, out of spite rather than from a more excusable fit of good taste, the Germans knocked it down. Came the victory, Lawrence and I were asked to put it up again but Mon Dieu at Quel Prix! So now it is the site of fruit machines and cafes with plastic flags, where once the English and Le Smoking reigned supreme.

TWO

Childhood

I cannot claim a wholly unhappy childhood, but by any standards mine had its bleak moments. Mama, faced with the task of bringing us up alone, was determined to be more the father than the mother, substituting toughness and constant reproach for affection and gentle restaint. She had only one passionate love and that was my father whom she continued to adore from afar. It seems to me a great mistake for anyone to cling to a love at a distance when proximity brings only rows and unhappiness. But she did just that.

I must have been a beautiful baby, for one of a procession of nurses sent my photograph up to a competition in a daily newspaper and I won. My mother gave the prize money to the NSPCC and the nurse got the sack. I had been born in 1915 and can still remember being taken to a cellar during an air-raid, but nobody believes me. I can also remember clearly a dreary series of sailor suits and fisticuffs with my brother whom I dearly loved. He was three years stronger than I and so always won – but they were hollow victories for we were invariably beaten for fighting.

Because of her toughness it was impossible for us to love Mama. We did not know then that, too proud to ask for alimony, it was a constant struggle for her to make ends meet, nor of her fears that, without a father's influence, we would turn into 'queers'. It is the constant reproaches and the beatings that stand out: beatings for persecuting flies, for rolling a half-crown down a London Street, for throwing a stone at a car, for biting my nails, for dirty ears, and always for wetting my bed – a disaster that persisted into adolescence and which was every bit as uncomfortable as the chastisement.

Not that we saw much of her, since we were looked after mainly by a kaleidoscope of nurses, governesses and tutors who produced us, brushed and combed, for our wiggings after tea. Mama was a great enthusiast and embraced each new preoccupation wholeheartedly; bridge, golf, tennis, the ukelele. Bezique, mah-jong and gin all had their turn; and always in an ever-changing series of cottages or hotels, both at home and abroad.

When the battle of education was nearly over she had a terrible car accident which deprived her of the use of an arm and put a stop to the tennis and the golf. With characteristic courage she threw herself into business with a publishing firm. Here she found two new and preoccupying enthusiasms, books and book-keeping. The first led to a collection of first editions and the second to a fascination for figures. The first editions were expensive but her enthralment with numerology had a far grimmer outcome. Her closeset friends began to show alarm at her fixations: that the figure four would bring the world to an end and that one was really two.

'Dorry is getting very odd,' they said, and of course, poor Dorry was.

Her desperate love for my father continued and the only time I saw her really happy was shortly before the outbreak of the Second World War when she heard from my father, then in Paris, that he wanted her to rejoin him. Wildly excited, she set off for a reunion she had craved for years. Two weeks later she returned – a violent lunatic.

We have never discovered what pushed her finally over the edge into bottomless despair. In Paris she found her beloved prostrate from drugs and the dope nurse in close attendance. Those whom the Gods wish so unfairly to destroy they first drive mad. She eked out her final fifteen frantic years in an expensive and soulless private home believing, happily at the end, that she was a dog. If only she had been able to stay in her London house, a merciful German bomb would have delivered her to a quicker peace – hers was the only building in the street to get a direct hit.

As was Mama's love unrequited so too was mine. When still quite small my affections, urgently in need of a focus, fastened on my godmother Midge, Marchioness of Tweeddale. Then in her fifties, she was the most beautiful creature I had ever seen and her Scottish home, Yester Castle, was a paradise. Yester had everything: dogs, dozens of them (how desperately I wanted one), cats, rats to hunt, bush babies, even monkeys. There were pheasants and grouse, game-keepers and guns. And there were salmon. There were so many keepers that one could even be spared to take out a small boy with an airgun in vain pursuite of a blackbird. Above all there was the half-hour after tea and the chance of seeing, and being with, Midge. At Christmas we children, masses of us there seemed to be, always got up a pantomime for the Magnificent Grown-Ups. Not a miserable little off-the-cuff do but carefully rehearsed on a real stage in the great hall, preceded by an overture by the Marquess's piper no less. At one such pantomime it was my ineffably proud part to present my godmother with flowers and say the words 'I love you very much'. So I did.

I treasured even her cigarette ends, captured from ash-trays and kept for years. She knew my childhood love and never snubbed it, and though there were many, many men who worshipped her, none could have been more ardent than this small boy.

How much of life that is lovely I learnt at Yester. The thrill of a gun pitted against a wary pigeon; the dozens of atomic trout that obliged the lure of my worms in mysterious holes of peaty water; the explosion of an unlucky salmon in my greatest triumph; beating for grouse and the one, permitted shot; the crumpets and the cakes; the tea and the blazing logs. And above all, the love that was nursed and cherished deep in my secret heart, the love which thrilled and hurt all at the same time.

And so to school.

St Peter's Court was the chosen preparation for Eton. My sole consolation was a catapult with which I had brought down a flying swallow at Yester, much to a watching gardener's – and my – astonishment. At school it had to be used surreptitiously and never with such success. A number of my missiles fell over the wall into the neighbouring girl's school. One found a chance mark on a pupil's head – fortunately she was more shocked than injured. At the ensuing inquest I owned up, got what I deserved, lost my catapult and gained a reputation for being a disaster.

School was utter agony. I couldn't sleep for the horror of the cold bath with which we had to start the day and the torment of my room-mates who inspected Kennard Minor's bed to see if he had wet it yet again. Nor could I work in the classroom for the thought of the misery of football in the afternoon. My sole and constant consolation was the carefully guarded tin full of Midge's cigarette ends.

On Sundays we walked in crocodile. On one such day some odious youth behind me alleviated his own boredom by seeing how often he could walk on my heels. To avoid this torture I stepped out into the road and got run over by a motor-bike. That, by the grace of the God of small boys was the end of my time at St Peter's Court. It was not my injuries that led to this final break, but that by my side-stepping breach of crocodile discipline I was adjudged as impossible to control.

My mother's chastisement was remarkably mild; in her own way perhaps she loved us, at least to the extent of drawing the line at her younger son being demolished by a motor-bike. She sent me next to another St Peter's, this time in Eastbourne where, although we still wore caps and blazers, my companion in the next-door bed ruined as many sheets as I and we had a cold bath only on Sundays.

One of the masters became my hero. He had been in the Royal Navy and gave exciting lantern-slide lectures on the Navy League. These instilled in me a splendid jingoism as well as intriguing me immensely by the clicking noises he made whilst changing the slides.

He had a very great influence on us all, but he must have been very peculiar (although I think harmless enough) for I remember him roaring with laughter at his own one little joke which was to make us recite very quickly, 'I chased a bug around the tree.' He would then exhort us urgently not to repeat this strange phrase outside his hearing. Apart from this apparent obsession with bugs he was an excellent teacher.

At my new St Peter's the deadly games of football and cricket were kept in a proportion which suited me better; boxing was accounted more important than either. On my first appearance in the ring I discovered that, being tall and skinny for my age, I had only to stick a long arm out to keep my opponent at bay. This was indeed a heaven-sent discovery; it made up for the bed-wetting even if it also meant that I was chosen to box for the school – an honour that I had certainly not sought and did not want.

During my first fight in this new and responsible role, I emerged from a petrified duck with such speed and vigour that, unseen by the referee, I knocked my opponent out with my head. I received my school colours and the approval of my mother – the only time that I can ever remember it. The most joyous outcome of this most dreadful foul was that I never got bullied again.

As the terms came and went so did the holidays; too seldom at Yester, too often trailing with tutors from hotel to hotel. At St Peter's I had at last become a dog among dogs; at Eton which came next, I again became a cur. Lawrence, who had preceded me there was shakily holding his own and I was to share a room with him.

I arrived for the first time at Eton with considerable panache. I was taken there by Rosa Lewis, dressed in embarrassing Edwardian flummery. She seemed to know all the boys' fathers, and just remembered on departure to say, 'Goodbye, dear boy!' My first impression of Eton was my astonishment at a routine whereby if one's housemaster, or M'Tutor as he was known, wished to administer a beating, he had to get the head-boy of the house to do it. As a fag I was constantly in trouble without ever really understanding why; as a pupil I had similar difficulty through my inability to compose Latin verse. This was a requirement every Thursday afternoon in what was called the Pupil Room. If one's effort failed as dismally as mine, reprisal in the form of a yellow ticket was issued. A number of these led to a white ticket and a ceremonial beating by the Lower Master. Such an occasion was known as a 'swiping', as opposed to the invariably more painful 'tanning' dispensed by the head-boy of the house. Swiping, though, was a terrifying psychological affair girt about with much ritual: a special menial held one down over a special block, whilst the special Lower Master beat one with a special birch. This performance cost the unfortunate parents an extra ten shillings on an already astronomical bill and was accounted for under the heading 'School Medicine'.

Three swipings were considered enough; a fourth was preempted by the sack. I avoided the latter by being asked to leave because apart from my other crimes I was now thought to be a thief.

The liberty given to the boys at Eton is, I am sure, one of the reasons for its undoubted greatness. It was also responsible for my final downfall. We were allowed to give tea-parties in our rooms and I was so delighted with my new-found friends – and with not being bullied – that I had determined to be generous, not easy or indeed possible as I saw it, on five bob a week. I had a brilliant and unselfish idea; I would gather up all the apparently unwanted books lying about the study I shared with my brother, take them down to the second-hand bookshop and flog the lot. I did so in a bag weighing heavily upon the shoulders of my Eton suit.

My bundle realized the not altogether generous sum of fifteen shillings, in fact a positively parsimonious amount, for among the volumes was a first edition of *Lady Chatterley's Lover*, pinched by Lawrence from our unsuspecting Tutor's rooms. The latter soon found this masterpiece on sale for £20 and traced the culprit, then basking in the aftermath of a tea-party unrivalled among fags. Kennard Minor was run to ground in the Pupil Room where, having given up the unequal struggle to produce that week's hexameter, he was engaged in delicately decorating Julius Caesar's bust with the ruder portions of the male anatomy.

This double crime put paid to what I think would have been a happy time at Eton. Then, as now, I thought the Tutor's decision a harsh one, but home I went to my mother where I became ill with diabetes. This proved to be a suitable and durable cover story for leaving and I have always been permitted to wear my only inheritance from my father – two Old Etonian ties, a blazer and a scarf.

The problem of my continued education was solved by the next holiday tutor who was also a housemaster at Cranleigh. He resolved to have me in his house as a day-boy and his wife would supervise my diet. Cranleigh patiently saw me through, and I must have done some work, for that considerable hurdle of yesterday's youth, the School Certificate, was skipped over with a bundle of credits including one for Divinity. Perhaps the hypnotist was responsible, for he had been detailed by my mother to give me a seance to ensure victory in my battle with the examiners and thus add merit to her case in her fight with my father over school fees. In the event we both won and there I was staring life in the face with a pocket full of certificates. No one has ever asked me for any of them.

THREE

Further Education in Europe

There was next to be a carefully pre-arranged first visit to my father, now on one of his rare trips to England. I was to impress him with my education so far and secure his future interest in my life.

I presented myself to him in the drawing room of the Cavendish Hotel, a dreadful youth in a loathsome blue suit and metal spectacles. He, flanked by Tallulah Bankhead and Rosa Lewis, regarded me with curiosity. They were all sipping champagne. I had never seen anything like them.

'And what, dear boy, do you most like doing?'

'Living in the country, ferretting and catching moles.'

There was a perceptible shiver from Miss Bankhead.

The visit was not a great success and was terminated early by my father who clearly had better things with which to engage his time; but it did result in an invitation to stay with him in Deauville for Le Gala due to take place the following week.

I was put up in the Hotel Normandie, Papa wisely remaining in the Hotel du Golf. We were to meet at midday at a fashionable café on the front. Here we would sip aperitifs whilst he graciously acknowledged the passing beau monde. Also in Deauville at that time was an Austrian emigré who sported little blue pants while running up and down the beach to get fit. He was shortly booked to become Lawrence's father-in-law and I found him approachable and affable. I was happily chatting to him on the first morning of my stay when

1. My grandfather, Sir George Barclay,
when His Majesty's Ambassador to Romania.

2. My father, Sir Coleridge Kennard, on the plage at Deauville with Berry Wall, an American habitue of the Casinos.

the fiacre containing Sir Coleridge arrived. Papa dismounted in full fig – impeccable dark suit, black homburg, pince-nez and spats.

'Good God,' said my new-found chum. 'Just look at the sort of Englishman who still comes to Deauville.'

When I told him that it was my father and they were about to become related, he fled, and Papa seeing him and the blue pants vanishing up the beach, remarked sadly,

'Just look at the sort of Englishman who comes here these days.'

Most evenings I reported to the Hotel du Golf and was made to listen after dinner to interminable Persian transcripts read out loud. None of them made any sense to me and my father sadly dismissed me as an unsophisticated lout.

Occasionally the pattern would change and we would motor miles in search of a special dish. I would generally eat in silence with my toes squirming in my shoes. One memorable evening he said:

'Tell me, George, have you ever had a woman?' The toes squirmed like mad. I hadn't and I wasn't even sure what they looked like without clothes. The facts of life had played no part in my schooling and I don't think until that moment I had given the matter much thought. My father, gazing reflectively at me, needed no reply.

'Ah,' he said. 'Ah, that explains a lot; we shall put the matter right tomorrow evening.' And so we did. The next evening we motored for more miles for more special dishes, but this time *à quatre*.

I was not as speechless as I feared for Mademoiselle (verging in age on Madame) was well briefed and listened attentively to my tales of moles and ferrets. Although she was not as attractive as my father's companion, we seemed to get on all right. I remember the initiation as being quick and having to wait endlessly for Papa – so long that we went back to our classroom and did it all again; this time with ferrets and moles forgotten. It was such fun that we kept Papa waiting and, miffed, he deemed the holiday over. There had been no talk of a career but I was to go to Switzerland to learn French.

At the time that The Lovely Lady Barclay married her Swiss Brigadier-General, I had acquired several French-Swiss relatives, each of them opulent, exclusive and enormously smug. They all lived in Geneva in their delightful chalets, ran a bank and copied assiduously the English Way of Life, drinking afternoon tea amongst appalling furniture and playing Bridge – not the revolutionary Contract but the much safer Auction.

Practically all of them had pretty daughters and there was nearly always an Uncle who was a Monsieur le Colonel or more, whose judgement at the Bridge table was final. Geneva was full of very correct young men and women students walking about with books under their arms and being as exclusive as their parents. It was as orderly and peaceful as the Lake itself – as the dowagers sailed from *soirée* to *soirée* so did the steamers paddle pompously from pier to pier.

I was to stay with Madame de Saugy, beautiful, motherly and the possessor of a most un-Swiss sense of humour. Like most of her friends she had a flat in the city and a chalet at the lake-side, where she made good wine and held *Les Cocktails* and *Les Thés*, the latter notable for the weight of *Chocolat*.

French was taught to me by Monsieur Thudicom, the very opposite of Madame, no sense of humour, tedious beyond belief behind his pince-nez. Of his teaching I remember only disconnected bits of *Le Cid: 'O rage, O désespoir . . .'* The battle-cry of angry young men down the ages, but in Geneva there were no angry young men, and that was a pity.

And yet, quite suddenly, the placid, law-abiding Genevois had their war. A machine-gun was unleashed in the main square and a number of people were hit. It was, I was assured, the work of a well-known Communist agitator whose name now struck terror into hitherto untroubled minds. 'Ah,' they sighed, 'if only we had someone like Monsieur Hitler in our government.'

Life soon resumed its even and tedious tenor. Thirty bob a week bought little fun and it was with relief that I was told by my father that as I could not begin to think of myself as educated until I spoke two languages; I was to be sent to Germany, to Frau von Mitzlaff.

Frau von Mitzlaff, whose name was Asta but who was always known as Mutte in the bosom of her extended family, was Madame de Saugy's sister. Before the Great War she had married a handsome Death's Head Hussar, Otto von Mitzlaff, and my mother, a great friend, had attended this wedding of the year. At the time, Otto was ADC to Little Willy, the Crown Prince, and there must have been more heel-clicking and medal-tinkling than at most, in that era of still splendid uniforms. Uniforms that were soon to be exchanged for khaki and field-grey and become the blood-soaked shrouds of their proud, now unsuspecting, wearers.

Otto, and his estates in Mecklenburg-Strelitz, were to survive this contest, although his pre-war eminence as Germany's leading race-horse owner had had to be modified to the extent that he was now a trainer as well. Mutte was doing her bit to help maintain the Schloss and its twenty servants, by taking in the adolescent children of her wide circle of international friends as paying guests. It was a splendid way of teaching her own children English and French, as well as the rest of us German and, of course, 'broadening all our views'. All this at a time when her own countrymens' views were being rapidly broadened by '*Unser liebe Adolf, ist er nicht wunderbar*?'

There were ten of us; Anne Elliot and I from England, Vincent and Jacqueline Paravicini, whose father was the Swiss Ambassador in London, a rather erratic Russian and an extremely well-developed Swiss girl with pigtails made up the guests to add to the von Mitzlaff children, Sven, Hubi, Moni and Daisy. A happy, carefree party who, by and large, obeyed Mutte's dictum; '*Meine liebe junge, aber Sie mussen immer Deutsch sprechen*,' if only because the autocratic Otto could hardly speak anything else. Autocratic he may have been, but he was a wonderful man with horses, spoke much common sense and earned our respect.

What a wonderful life it was. Every day we would ride out on the race-horses, Waldmeister, Nobelmann, Escamillo and many others, three or four strings of them and all improving under the master's hand and eye. We would ride through the pine forests accompanied by the yearlings, the mares and even the foals, all running loose. We were quick to obey Otto's orders for on our good behaviour and management of our charges depended our chance of getting a gallop that day. The training gallops were cut on sandy soil through fields of barley and woods of pine. In winter we used the frozen lake with its thick and cushioning layer of snow over the ice. The lake served a purpose in summer too, for then we would ride the horses in and swim them for half an hour. These methods produced the winning stable year after year.

There were other delights to add to the horses and the company we kept. At night fallow deer and boar crept out of the forest to feed. At such places hides were built high up in the pines from which with a rifle we were able to add to the already bountiful larder. Not great sport, nor even very sporting, but executed in beauty as the orange sun dipped below the trees to be replaced by the moon, and in the company of a lovely girl, still in her riding clothes and nervous at the noises of the night. For we were all falling in and out of love each varying week and there was the walk home and the kisses in the dark. We were fit and young, there was laughter and beauty and our cares were few. But as we rode and shot and laughed and loved, the shadows were gathering again over that great country.

Into the villages came the handsome young men in their

brown shirts. There were bands once more and stirring music where for long there had been poverty in the aftermath of war. Even the stable lads went out and bought their shirts and the belts with the motto '*Gott mit Uns*'. The songs at the fests changed from talk of love and the countryside to the menacing growls of '*Die Fahne Hoch*' and the rest.

All this had an astonishing effect on the Swiss girl with the nice proportions and the pigtails, for on the day that the head lad received the gold stripe of the *Stürmbannführer*, she succumbed, both to him and to the lure of the *Hitler Mädchen* uniform and her now free hair flew in the wind. None of us took her shooting any more and she married her *Stürmbannführer* when he became the local *Gauleiter*.

The Führer from Berlin spoke often on the wireless and Mutte, that most gentle of her sex, would rush us through our dinner so that the servants might assemble in the great hall to listen, as households in England might have listened to the King at Christmas. What gibberish he ranted! It was hard for we guests not to laugh, but we could not. We loved that household and Mutte, and there she sat entranced, nodding her head, applauding at intervals and with tears in her eyes as the final torrent of words reached its crescendo and gave way to the massed bands and '*Deutschland Uber Alles*' and '*Die Fahne Hoch*'. Here the servants joined in and Mutte tried too, but she didn't know the words – anymore than she and millions like her realized the implications.

The rest of the family reacted in hugely differing ways. Otto von Mitzlaff, the ex-regular soldier, former ADC to the Kaiser to be, the best of sportsmen, generous loser, modest winner, would opt out before such occasions, giving his wife a little hug and retiring to his study with a rueful smile that may have contained a hint of amused contempt.

Sven, the eldest, had inherited his father's good looks and sporting instincts. Older than any of us, he was already commissioned into a cavalry regiment and appeared, much to the delight of the girls, for odd weekends and some longer leaves. There was little difference between his attitudes and those I was to come across later in similar British regiments. He and his friends thought Hitler was a joke, and yet perhaps, not quite:

'He's hardly the thing, of course, but he has done the Fatherland quite a bit of good.'

Sven was the champion jockey of Germany and we were able to cheer him on at a number of race-meetings. He didn't get away much, apart from racing, because his regiment was busy mechanizing. On this subject he was silent.

Remaining silent was something of which the younger son, Hubi, was incapable. Hubi was a nasty piece of work. Younger than most of us, he was still at school and keenly immersed in all the fanatical panoply of the Hitler Youth. Self-importantly he carried files marked 'Secret', and these we regularly stole and examined. They contained official Nazi dogma, full of the most vicious hatreds and incitements. One day we tired of Hubi's strutting and threw him into the lake. He minded very much but the rest of the family seemed not to object, or indeed be surprised. Later, in the heady days of '*Wir fahren nach England*' and now in the *Lüftwaffe*, he was shot down and killed.

The girls, carried along on the tide of events and social pressures, joined the *Hitler Mädchen* in an unenthusiastic sort of way, treating the whole business as a joke. But even on them the Führer was capable of exercising a powerful effect. We used to travel far to race-meetings and once we went to Berlin. There was a Nazi rally one evening and we attended, along with what seemed to be the whole population of the capital. Hitler was due to arrive at ten; we stood in the darkened arena waiting as the tension mounted and sharpened. Suddenly he was there; to a million '*Ach, Mein Gotts*' he stepped on to the stage as ten thousand lights blazed and a thousand banners waved. The massed brown-shirted arms shot into the air and the '*Sieg Heils*' deafened the dead. A pin-drop hush fell on the worshipping multitude as the little man began to speak. He held that throng as surely as any puppet-master holds his marionettes. He whispered, cajoled and screamed and they were with him all the way. Even Daisy, the carefree Daisy, began to blub and Moni didn't speak to me for a week when I told her that I wished her race had been brought up, not on Siegfried, but on Ferdinand the Bull. The final blow for me that night was to be told that the buses had been ordered off the roads so that we could all go home singing Nazi marching songs. We had miles to walk.

I returned to England, happy in my friends, mature in body but politically bemused. I little suspected the final outcome of the mass hysteria I had witnessed as a nation was reborn.

FOUR

The Last Years of Peace

By this time I had acquired a taste for education and had passed the examination known as Little Go for entry into Trinity College, Cambridge. I went to look at the rooms allotted to me and liked them very much. Sadly, it was not to be; my mother and father now entered upon one of their worst long-distance financial wrangles and it was decided that they could not afford an undergraduate; I would have to get a job. I chose this moment to apply, quite mildly, to my father for an increase in my thirty shillings a week allowance; he was not sympathetic and told me that at my age he expected me to support him. I was uncertain how to go about this; neither of my parents had any influence in the City – indeed they held it in the scorn customary at that time.

My life was further complicated by the social requirement to do the Season – an orgy of afternoon teas, cocktail parties and dances organized by my mother's friends for their debutante daughters. I had no objection to this; the hostesses of the day engaged in the keenest possible rivalry to produce prodigious dinners, and I was thus able to dispense with lunches altogether. The price to be paid was the need to be endlessly charming and attentive to the, often, unattractive focus of the evening and her friends; but it helped stretch out my thirty bob.

Occasionally it was possible to lure a promising and pretty partner away from her chaperone and into the dare-devil atmosphere of a night-club, but such a proceeding too often ended in a request for a Declaration of Intent, and that was the moment to bolt. In any case, my meagre resources allowed few such ventures and I was still besotted by Jacqueline Paravicini. We had solemnly vowed eternal loyalty to each other in Germany and she was now Deb of the Year. This had obviously gone to her head and she was constantly being trotted out by a string of strange young men called Guards Officers. I hardly got a look in, possibly because I couldn't afford taxis and she rapidly tired of having to walk home in a £300 dress.

In a desperate effort to generate more cash I took a job with Miss Marty Mann's News Agency just behind the Strand. Miss Mann was a friend of Mama's and started me off on two pounds a week, a sum which helped considerably with the taxis but, alas, Jacqueline had drifted out of reach. The News Agency was supposed to teach me journalism but was inclined to give me little more to do than stick on stamps and, occasionally, use my friends. I was, for instance, persuaded to ask the Marquess of Tweeddale to pose in Daks trousers. He was not amused.

After many weeks of stamp sticking I was sent to the Old Bailey to gain experience while covering a murder trial. I scribbled away earnestly – and rather more slowly than the short-hand knowledgeables around me. I gradually became aware that the nice, respectable woman sitting beside me spent a great deal of time sobbing into her handkerchief. She turned out to be Mrs Hicks whose husband Reginald had, it seemed, on the evidence quite understandably, shoved his mother-in-law into a gas-oven. It took the jury no time at all to convict and the judge donned his black cap to pronounce sentence. This, not unnaturally, upset Mrs Hicks even more and I took her home in a taxi. Before leaving her to her sorrows I impressed upon her that I would place my vast experience as a journalist at her disposal should she feel I could be of any help. She telephoned within days. Would I come round at once? She had proof that he husband hadn't done it. In view of what I'd heard in court this seemed surprising, but, hot on the scent of a scoop, I went round. The 'proof' consisted only of a letter from the condemned cell repeating that he was innocent and adding a wealth of circumstantial waffle that I had not heard at the Old Bailey. Could something be done? You bet it could!

I took the letter, cancelled my evening's dancing, and wrote an impassioned plea aimed at publication in the *Daily Express*. All my frustrated, journalistic talents and, indeed, my heart went into that piece proclaiming the wretched Reginald's innocence. In the early hours I rushed round to the *Express* with my masterpiece and the corroborative letter. Yes, the Editor would take it. I went home secure in the knowledge that I had made my national press debut and saved a man's life. I could hardly sleep as I waited for the morning papers. I seized the *Express*; there it was on the front page. But not a word of my article; just Reginald's letter under the headline: 'Handwriting of a Guilty Man'. Fortunately I neither saw nor heard from the unfortunate Mrs Hicks again but idealism flew out of the window. To hell with journalism.

In a disappointed dream I found myself pausing at an Army Recruiting Office window and gazing at a poster showing a Guards Officer in full dress. No wonder Jacqueline was impressed; that's what I would do. So I went in, filled up a form and went home to break the good news to Mama. She had a fit. What had I done? Didn't I know that I had joined as an Other Rank (whatever that was), probably for life, and I was bound to be court-martialled?

'Do you really want to join the Army?'

'Yes I think so.'

Well, then, she would ring up an old friend who was commanding the Bays . . .

By so simple an expedient she aborted my attempted foray into the Foot Guards and in next to no time I appeared, dithering with fright, as a Second Lieutenant of the Army Supplementary Reserve, in the Officer's Mess of the Queen's Bays at Aldershot. It was a Sunday and the only person I met was a splendid figure in the uniform known as Blues. I gave him a staggering version of what I believed to be a salute and he told me that he was the Mess Sergeant Major.

The life of an Officer on the Supplementary Reserve was not secure. The Reserve was designed to produce a pool of Officers who could be called upon in an emergency. There was no formal training at an Officer Cadet School or Sandhurst; it was all done on the job during attachment to a regular regiment. I was made a supernumerary Troop Leader, which meant that I was put under an experienced Sergeant whose duty it was to pass on to me such knowledge as he had and stop me making too much of an ass of myself in public. I was very much in awe of him and it was some time before he was able to convince me that it was he who saluted me first and it was I who should be called 'Sir'.

Later he was to give me sobering advice, which was to stay with me all my life. In a slight altercation I said to him, 'I suppose you think that I'm a c-t, Sergeant'. 'Nothing as useful as that, Sir . . .' A delightful man, alas killed later in Italy.

My world now consisted of three NCOs, five Troopers, sixteen horses and Ryan, my batman. When he was allotted to me I was told that if I could command Trooper Ryan successfully I could command anybody, but I doubt whether Field-Marshal Montgomery himself could have commanded Ryan successfully. Nevertheless he was part and parcel of My Troop, and we were part of the squadron and that, in turn, was part of the Regiment. So it was, so it always has been and so, God willing, it always will be – the regimental family, the team.

Germany had taught me to love the horse but it hadn't prepared me for the hard life of a horsed regiment. I had glimpsed something of it through Sven's eyes – as I had also glimpsed the tanks on the secret training grounds. But in Aldershot, starting at 5.30, we were at it all day: riding school, musketry and sword drill. Wrists, back and shoulders all ached and we were convinced in our tired but euphoric fitness, that no enemy, mechanized or otherwise, could stand up to the Queen's Bays when they were having a go.

As we worked so did we play. Our pay was ten shillings a day and our Mess Bills not less than fifteen. There were unexpected expenses too, such as those arising from furniture unable to stand up to the rigours of after-dinner Mess polo and occasional forays to London. But against this continuing economic failure were set the immeasurable benefits of duty. It was, for example, a duty to hunt troop horses in Leicestershire, a duty to take two months' leave to do so and a duty to play polo on troop horses in the summer. Thus was the cavalry spirit bred and nourished; the spirit that has survived through wars great and small, and remained unconquered in victory and defeat.

I loved the life and determined to make it my own. In order to regularize my position I went to a crammers at Farnham where I swotted diligently at Tactics, Current Affairs, Military Organization and Administration – the subjects required for the Army examination. It was mostly common-sense and what was not was learnt easily by heart. I had no great difficulty in passing, and having done so, had the great good fortune to be gazetted to His Majesty's 4th Queen's Own Hussars.

Life in the 4th Hussars was very like that in the Bays but now I knew I belonged; this was my family, this was the rest of my life. The regimental spirit is hard to define but is born out of a selflessness that those who have not experienced it find hard to understand. The outer trappings which bind the whole together alter with changing standards and expectations, but the inner core remains – the certainty (shared with every similar regiment) that your regiment is the best; the bonds which bring back hundreds every year to regimental reunions, and above all the readiness to die, not to save the country but not to let the Regiment, the Family, down. Such concepts are now alien to most, and perhaps were so then to the majority of civilians, but those self-same civilians were soon to join us and become as bitten as the bit.

Meanwhile we took such abstract notions for granted and lived life to the full – the manoeuvres on Laffan's Pain, the inter-Troop competitions, the drills, the hunting, the polo and the trips to London. Here, if one happened to be flush, one took the girl of one's choice to the Four Hundred; sometimes on to the Cavendish, but usually one 'had to behave'. Frustrating. But frustration did not apply to the Bag of Nails. This night club, run by Millie, was the second Guards and Cavalry Club. Full of pretty girls, it was the scene of many happy hours of enthusiasm and delights. Some of the girls happily married their partners, others gave all they had with abandon, even free of charge. The little cigarette girl, whose generosity of lovely body, though perhaps not of mind, will forever be in my thoughts. And Millie was to send Christmas Cards to all of us throughout the war. And then the frantic dash to Aldershot, for first parade. All these while the storm clouds gathered over us until we, too, felt the first tremors of what was to follow: we were to be mechanized. The wits in the Cavalry Club summed it up: no longer were we to love and ride away, but rather to screw and bolt. Hard as it was for the old sweats to come to terms with the loss of their beloved horses, it was harder still to master the perversities of early carburettors. But we managed, even if some still insisted on polishing every piece of piping in already gleaming internal combustion engines.

The Regiment had, as its models, the 11th Hussars and the 12th Lancers, already mechanized for some years. The honour of the regiment was at stake; we would do it better, better than anyone. At first we had 15cwt trucks as substitutes for tanks, and red flags for anti-tank guns. We bucketed about the Wiltshire plains in our lorries, pointing them, like horses, at obstacles; on Hampshire roads we charged road-blocks, unwilling to stop for red flags. Watched one day, unbeknown to me, by a gaggle of visiting military attachés accompanied by British generals, my Troop was happily engaged in rounding up a covey of partridges, the trucks performing astonishing antics in the process. The visitors' field-glasses were not powerful enough to see the birds and the lorries' manoeuverings interested them greatly, particularly the German who was convinced that he had stumbled upon a new and potentially lethal armoured warfare tactic.

The tanks soon arrived, the Mark VIB, light and shod with tracks. Farriers, saddlers, even cooks got down to learning about this new machine. It was a time for sound, encouraging leadership, and this we got from Lieutenant-Colonel Scott-Cockburn, the famous Scottie, a brilliant horseman and winner of the Kadir Cup, the Blue Riband of pig-sticking in India, three times. If he could throw himself so seriously and wholeheartedly into this new method of warfare, then so could we. Munich came and went. All leave was stopped and we trained constantly; it was clear now for what.

FIVE

Wavell and War

The General Officer Commanding Southern Command from his Headquarters in Aldershot later became Field-Marshal Lord Wavell. A brilliant brain, a huge appetite for work, a fine commander, sportsman and poet, Wavell was uncompromising in his dealings with the world. Mindful always of what he termed the 'butcher's bill', he later fell out with his political masters, including two Prime Ministers. We adored him.

The Commanding Officer sent for me one day and told me that the great man was to become GOC Middle East and wanted me as his ADC. The Colonel naturally had agreed – it was, as he saw it, both an honour for the Regiment and a welcome relief from Kennard. I, for my part, did not want to leave at a time when we were training so hard for the war we all knew was inevitable, but it seemed unwise to turn down this wonderful chance to see how the other half lived and worked.

Wavell was a silent man, not given much to small talk, and certainly not with his ADC; it was not until our arrival at the Gare du Nord in Paris on the first stage of our journey to Cairo, that he turned to me and said: 'I can't call you Loopy in front of General Gamelin; haven't you got a proper name?' Seldom in the Army had I been called George, and never since.

The Middle East was a huge command and woefully unprepared for modern warfare; Khartoum, then our biggest oil depot, had few guns and no ammunition; other vitally strategic places had ammunition and no guns. We flew far and wide; to Syria and Beirut to see General Weygand and to Sidi Barrani to see Captain Abdul, a magnificently aggressive Sudanese who wished only to be allowed to take on the whole Italian army single-handed. Not so General Weygand who, from the depths of a comfortable arm-chair in the best hotel in Beirut, declared that he would need five divisions to defeat the Italians should war be declared; ten to contain them if they announced neutrality; and fifteen if they became allies, to extricate them from whatever mess they got themselves into. We flew to Aden to confer on HMS *Warspite*, dressed overall, magnificent and invincible, of whom Admiral Cunningham once said, 'There is no doubt that when the old lady lifts her skirts she can run'! Later we flew to Jerusalem, where Generals Wavell and Barker (and their aides) were shot at on the terrace of the King David Hotel. And always we flew in that dreariest of aircraft, the Vickers Valencia – 100 miles an hour with a following wind – and a reliability record which compared unfavourably with the Mark VIB tank; we crashed three times, twice in the desert and once in Palestine.

On our rare visits to his Headquarters in Cairo and Alexandria, the General was wont to test the flimsy civil defences and black-out procedures; it was my task to initiate such exercises. The first, at Alex, resulted in 123 murders and, in Cairo, King Farouk fell down the steps of his palace when the lights went out.

I had thought that the Declaration of War would have had an incisive definity, and so I suppose it did in England. In Cairo it all seemed rather long drawn-out. I quote from my diary, in which had recorded the following bit of doggerel, but I can no longer remember who was its author.

> 30 Aug 1939
> The news looks bad now. If it improves we go
> to the Sudan on Saturday. If not I shall make

every effort to get back to the Regiment. It will not be pleasant forming up to the General and asking permission to leave him, but, fascinating as this job is, I do not think that it is the place for a regimental officer in war.

1 Sep

We have just heard that the Gauleiter of Danzig finds what he calls the preposterous behaviour of the Poles too much, and rumour has it that Hitler has decided to march.

'Twas Danzig, and the Swastikoves
Did Heil and swagger in the Reich.
All Nazi were the Lindengroves
And the Neuraths Julesstreich.

Beware the Grabberwoch, my son,
And plans that spawn the plots that hatch.
Beware the Jawjaw bird, and shun
The furious Bundessnatch.

He took his Aryan hordes in hand,
Long time Gestapo-taught.
Then rested he by the Baltic Sea
And stood awhile in thought.

Then at the Polish state he swore,
The Grabberwoch with eyes aflame
Came goering down the corridor
And goebelled as it came.

Eins zwei, eins zwei, one in the eye
For Polska folk. Alas, alack;
He left them dead and as their head
He came Meinkampfing back.

'Now I have got my Lebensraum,
Come to my arms my Rhenish boy.
Oh brabjous day, Seig Heil, Hurray'.
He exulted in his joy.

'Twas Danzig and the Swastikoves
Did Heil and swagger in the Reich,
All Nazi were the Lindengroves
And the Neuraths Julesstreich

What is the reaction at home, one wonders? Here people are bored by the war of nerves. We hear so many rumours and so few facts. Post from England has stopped. I suppose tomorrow we shall be at war.

2 Sep
We have just received reports that Germany attacked Poland at 5.45 yesterday morning. I have been on duty all day and there has been no message from either the Government or the War Office. We got the news from Reuter's. Cairo is excited and the police are carrying gas masks. Every hotel is full of 'key' personnel who arrived on HMS *Shropshire*. 2000 of them on a ship designed for 700. A Guards officer made a killing, buying up all the lilos in Malta and selling them on board.

3 Sep
We are at war and there is great relief that the waiting is over. No excitement here but a bad moment when we heard that London had been bombed. Gloom dispelled a little later on hearing that it was a false alarm. We are standing-by to fly to Turkey to sign a pact. The

only other news of note is that we have captured the *Bremen*.

Turkey vacillated over that particular agreement and we did not go. Instead we flew to Baghdad and there was a conference in the grounds of the British Embassy where the sky was blotted out by clouds of bats taking off from the Tigris. Then a fascinating dinner with a number of Iraqi politicians who looked as if they would like to murder each other. Quite soon after we left they did just that.

On another occasion we had to attend a most important conference in Beirut with General Weygand to which we flew downwind at 100mph in our Vickers Valencia. It was due to last three days. Our RAF pilot asked me if he could fly back to Cairo in the interim. Unfortunately I said Yes. More unfortunately, the Anglo-French conference was a flop and my General decided to fly back next day. Affable goodbyes, ceremonial conduct to the airport, inspection outside the aerodrome of a guard of honour of Spahis, and me, the ADC, knowing that on the tarmac would no plane!

'Allo, 'allo, *Quelle blague*. But with infinite courtesy General Weygand offered us his private plane. Air France, with upholstered seats.

'Loopy, that's the best thing you've ever done,' my General said.

We returned to Cairo where Said, the magnificent butler at Government House, handed Wavell a letter from the Military Secretary. He opened it and looked at me long and hard. It was my recall to England and the Regiment. The aircraft back to England could not travel fast enough for me but when it arrived I found life a dreadful anticlimax and soon regretted not heeding Wavell's advice: 'Stay on here in Egypt. If you don't you'll only stay in England until your Regiment comes here.'

There have been excellent biographies of the late Field-Marshal Lord Wavell, to which I can add nothing but my appreciation of a brilliant brain, a huge capacity for work and a fine commander. Most of the battles of the war were won by numbers and equipment; Lord Wavell won his with neither – and always at variance with the politicians. 'Take the blame and don't complain' was his philosophy as a soldier. As Viceroy he departed from it once. On receiving a message from Mr Attlee complaining that the Viceroy's policy differed greatly from that of His Majesty's Government, he cabled back: 'It is impossible for the Viceroy's policy to differ from that of His Majesty's Government, since His Majesty's Government does not have a policy. That is my complaint. Wavell.'

His final bitterness was yet to come – the death of his only son, Archie John, killed on active service in Kenya by the Mau Mau.

We were stationed on Lord Hotham's place in Yorkshire with very little to do except maintain the estate in the enforced absence of most of his Lordship's workforce. There was a severe petrol shortage and for the most part our tanks were immobile. Our only warlike action was to stand-to at dawn each day to repel any parachute attack. There were no attempted landings in Yorkshire, although a parachutist did drop in on the Marquess of Tweeddale at Yester, to be greeted by the one remaining keeper and delivered to the sole indoor servant, an elderly cook. She inspected his fingernails, found them clean and manicured and pronounced him a gentleman. He spent a few formal moments with the Marquess before being collected by the constabulary.

Tedious as life was for we regular soldiers, it was infinitely more chafing for those that had been called up into the

Regiment to make us up to our war strength. Staring up into an empty sky for a few shillings a week, whilst small businesses in many parts of England struggled to make ends meet in the care of wives and parents, was not a recipe for high morale, especially as mail was erratic and the most innocent of letters was subject to zealous censorship. We had fifty tanks, (soon to be reduced to forty-eight by two Polish Officers who, allotted some of our precious petrol for familiarization training, succeeded only in crashing into each other), but we were seldom allowed to use them.

Life was equally bemusing for the wartime Officers, among whom was Randolph Churchill, whose father had served in the Regiment before the turn of the century. Politically active and severely critical of the Chamberlain government, he was more frustrated than most. Fortunately he was a keen bridge player and there was no shortage of time in which to play. Equally fortunately he was phenomenally bad at the game and many a poorer Officer's mess bill was subsidized in this way.

Rumours still abounded, including one that we were to be shipped to Norway to help the Finns fight off Hitler's newest ally, Stalin. Many formed up asking for leave to go to the French Alps to learn to ski! This was, of course refused. Instead we were all sent to Market Harborough. It seemed odd that we, the possessors of some of the few tanks left in England, should be sent as far from the coast as it was possible to be when the air was thick with talk of invasion from across the Channel, but we did our best to accept our lot and enjoy life as best we could. Love was in the air as it always is when war is imminent, and many marriages started there – mine included. There is a time in everyone's life when time stands still. Just for a few seconds, on a bridge, in the moonlight in a Northamptonshire village the world stopped for me. Promises were made, the bottomless promises of youth. A wedding followed and a daughter conceived, whom I was not to see for four years. There were a few glorious weeks before the loveliest girl in the world was left alone. 'Parting is such sweet sorrow'? Not a bit of it, plain bloody misery after so little time.

Before we left, Billy Hornby and I had one last hunt together in the Shires. He was that special friend among all my friends, with whom I had shared horses, money, girlfriends and good times. What a day it was but when would the next one be, and when would I see my Cecilia again? None of us knew as the train drew out of that dark Midlands station that the journey was to last four years, and none of us knew our immediate destination. Wavell had been right!

We joined our ship at Liverpool, one of many such liners which, with the grey escorts, sailed for Egypt. It seemed strange to sail west to go south but we were routed almost to America before turning for South Africa. For the first time serious homesickness set in among the vast majority who had never been away from home before and who were now bereft of even the most spasmodic mail. In Durban we were decanted on a population enthusiastic in its wish to be hospitable but totally unprepared for the excesses of this expeditionary force. There was still no mail; if there had been, a number of those incidents, born as they were out of worry and apprehension, might well have been avoided. There was a lesson there for the hard-pressed welfare services.

We disembarked finally, with our tanks, at Port Said and drove to a collection of tents lying in the desert. This was Tahag Camp, and there was still no mail. Wavell's offensive had started with success and we engaged frantically in fitting our Mark VIBs with desert modification kits and painting them in yellow camouflage, hoping to be in on the kill. Our Commanding Officer, now Barney Lillingston, asked me to go to GHQ, see the General and beg that we should be employed as soon as the tanks were ready. I found my old chief calm and thoughtful as hourly reports of success rolled in. It would, it seemed, be too late to get us in on the battle but he told me: 'You will be used shortly and you won't like it.' He was right. The next day we received orders to remove the desert camouflage and modifications and paint the tanks green. The troops had a word for it and wondered what next.

Billy Hornby and I got permission to go up to the front lines to gain some battle experience. We gained euphoric and totally false impression of what war was all about by being greeted everywhere we went by Italians anxious to surrender – until we came to a beach where we thought we would bathe; there the water was full of jostling Italian corpses – the inelegant result of the sinking of a prison ship.

On our return to Tahag, we found the long-awaited mail and an enterprising regimental bookie laying odds on our next destination. Greece was 5 to 1.

Since Billy and I were by now battle-hardened veterans by dint of our few days' visit to the front, the Colonel appointed us to take the tanks and their drivers on a landing craft to Piraeus; the rest of the Regiment was to travel on the ill-fated HMS *Gloucester*. Once embarked we were alarmed to note that not only was the Captain of our ship clearly in the shaking grip of advanced DTs, but we had no Royal Navy escort. It occurred to us that the two facts were probably connected; but somehow we got there and so did the *Gloucester*. We were exhorted to unload at speed as the swiftness of our deployment might alter the whole course of the war. An interested observer at the quayside was the German military attaché to Greece, making the most of the fact that those two countries were not yet at war. Doubtless his copious notes reflected the facts that the Mark VIBs were the self-same tanks that Churchill had assured Parliament would never be required to face the Germans again after the Dunkirk débâcle, and that the more modern Cruisers of the 3rd Royal Tank Regiment, who were with us, had no spare parts and could not go into action until they arrived. We got on a train for Salonika amidst waves of cheering Greeks, pressing us with bunches of flowers and bottles of ouzo.

We never quite got to Salonika, getting off at Veroia some 40 miles west. The country was wild and mountainous and it was so cold that it snowed. We were glad that we had disobeyed the orders given to us by Cairo that we should give up our battledress and sail for Greece in khaki drill.

We continued to move north and west as the battle lines were drawn. The Greek, Australian and New Zealand Divisions formed the main defence, whilst we and the rest of the 1st Light Armoured Brigade operated in front of them to try and identify the enemy's intentions. The attack began on 6 April, 1941, and the first of our casualties were our anti-aircraft crews as we constantly adjusted our positions in response to the changing situation. It began to rain and Clem, my squadron leader, held frequent conferences under his red golfing umbrella. He had a passion for hunting over the huge walls and dank ditches of his native Ireland and a terrible temper; the men of the Squadron loved both the man and his imaginative cursing. At the conclusion of each conference he would cheerfully proclaim: 'Let he that hath no stomach for this fight, depart.' Quite where we were to go he did not elaborate but it impressed us all with its seriousness and we returned to our tanks determined to improve our camouflage and polish up our gunnery drills.

The Adolf Hitler SS Division found us at first light. Nose to tail, their monstrous panzers edged slowly up the winding mountain road towards our positions. At a little bridge and fully visible to me, they stopped and sent one of their number lumbering forward to reconnoitre. There was a sharp hiss of indrawn breath from my gunner: 'Better not fire yet Sir, they might fire back.'

But we did, and so did most of the squadron on the hill. Our fire was accurate but appeared to do little damage as the tank slowly withdrew to rejoin its fellows. It took them over an hour to move again and then very cautiously; little did they know that, with their superior armour and firepower, they could have brushed us aside like flies. The American military observer with the German forces (the USA was not yet in the war) recorded that the 'advance was held up by the brilliant use of the British armoured forces'.

Later that day I heard Clem speaking through my fading wireless set: 'Look out Loopy, there are some German infantry. Come with me. Charge.'

Charge we did, in hot pursuit, and then my tank lost a track as my Squadron Leader faded into the distance. Not wishing to be abandoned, I tried to get him on the radio but by now it had failed completely so I drew his attention in the only way open to me: I fired at his turret with my machine-gun. Hat, map and binoculars all flew overboard as he turned to meet this attack from an unexpected quarter. His language when he finally understood the situation was surpassed only by that he used to me later that night when he discovered that my tank had been demolished by enemy fire. Luckily my whole crew survived and we were rescued by one of the Troop Leaders, John de Moraville; on that day John won an MC.

Of all the military operations, withdrawal is the most difficult, and of the roles of the component parts of an army in retreat, that of the rearguard is the worst. Worst because there is always a shortage of fuel, of spares, of sleep, of food and always there is the enemy harrying you from the ground and from the air, all day and all night. Our role in the withdrawal of the allied expeditionary force in the face of overwhelming superiority in all departments except guts was that of rearguard.

The *Luftwaffe* had never had it so good. Every southward mountain road was full of slow-moving targets and we could not abandon our vehicles during the raids, since, by doing so we would block the route of others. Very little could be done for the wounded; nothing could be done for my Troop

Corporal, who, with little left of his neck and choking on his blood, whispered to me: 'What'll become of my poor missus now?'

We reached the Peloponnese, where we hoped we might be allowed to stand and fight. By now the Squadron had a seventy-mile front from Corinth to Patras, four tanks, a handful of trucks and a hundred men. Here there was a respite as the enemy, too, had its resupply troubles. All went quiet apart from the plane that machine-gunned Billy and me as we clung to one motor-cycle on a mountain pass. What a sleep we had that night in the olive groves, but at dawn bigger aircraft appeared and the parachutists dropped like autumn leaves as the Germans tried to seize the bridge over the canal. We took a heavy toll of them but they got on to the bridge and our Sappers tried to blow it. Nothing happened and on they came, accompanied by a news-reel truck filming for the benefit of Berlin cinema audiences. Then up it went, bridge, trucks, troops and camera. Whoopee!

Close to that bridge, the Colonel and the Adjutant, returning from Headquarters with fresh orders, ran into an ambush; for them the war was over. Clem took command and on we went, what was left of us, to Kalamata, Greece's most southerly port. There we were to be embarked to fight another day. As we set off, Billy Hornby was captured. Later he was to be put into a POW cage in Salonika where he saw his chance to make a run for it. They spotted him; a few pfennigs worth of German powder and that bundle of gaiety and fun lay dying – dead. *Ja*, he was shot while trying to escape.

A few miles from Kalamata we paused while Clem went on to try and discover what the powers that be, if there were any, wanted us to do. We were out on our feet and, one by one, we collapsed by the side of the road in sleep, some thirty men and one anti-tank rifle, grimly clutched by Trooper Small. I awoke to the sound of machine-gun fire and of John de Moraville exhorting Small to fire at a German armoured car. He did his best but the bolt jammed. I ran to a garden shed inside which were more of our men; I told them to beat it quickly to the south. I badly wanted to go with them but couldn't leave John and Small. The volume of firing increased as I did my best to retain my dignity; as I arrived John was trying to kick the gun into action; suddenly he spun round and said: 'The buggers shot me,' and so they had. In his neck was a neat entry hole and no exit; it didn't seem to affect him much, except to increase the volume of oaths he was directing at the enemy as the gun still refused to fire. I was trying to plug the wound with a handkerchief when a polite, Teutonic voice, speaking in a modulated English accent informed me that we were now prisoners of war. It was my turn to spin round. I gaped: 'Good God, Otto, *wie gehts*? What on earth are you doing here?' It was Otto Hertzog who had often come to stay at the von Mitzlaffs and was their cousin.

Otto's men were busy rounding up the remainder of our party, including those who had bolted from the garden shed; three had been killed in the initial burst of fire. We were all shepherded together on the road and I tried to introduce Otto to John. The latter threw his field-glasses on to the ground and said: 'For God's sake Loopy stop talking to that bloody German.' I suddenly realized that I might appear to be some sort of fifth-columnist and contented myself with trying to find out what would happen to us now. Otto told me that we were to be taken to Kalamata by vehicle and from there sent to a prison camp. We would be well treated and John would be taken to hospital. He added that he would take me out to dinner when he had some leave. All this seemed good news; Kalamata was, as far as we knew, full of British troops still fighting, and it should be relatively easy to make a break when we arrived there. We were put into an open truck and driven off singing 'Roll Out the Barrel' at the tops of our voices; this seemed to annoy the German escort considerably. We redoubled our vocal efforts.

The Germans appeared to have no clue how many British and allied troops there were in Kalamata, or perhaps because they thought that most by this time were unarmed, they didn't care. We drove on into the outskirts of the town in the gathering dusk and were fired on. We were bundled into a cellar and I decided that this was my moment. As I gathered up my courage, I heard shouted German orders for the deployment of a large field gun which was to begin firing shells on to the beaches now packed with largely unarmed troops waiting for the naval evacuation. Our guard dropped dead, shot by one side or the other and I hopped it. There was some erratic shooting from both sides as I ran down the street and eventually I found myself among some New Zealanders. I explained that I knew the whereabouts of the gun that was even now causing havoc and death on the beaches and a Sergeant said: 'Right, Sir, hop into this truck and we'll go get him.' The truck was a small one and Sergeant Hinton had only a revolver; I was unarmed. I had just started to mutter, 'Not bloody likely . . .' and other excuses when I was elbowed aside by a huge Australian. 'Come on then Taffy,' said Sergeant Hinton, and off they charged, straight at the gun. But it wasn't the only gun, it was supported from both flanks by automatic weapons. There was a vast commotion, then silence – the gun lying on its side and the truck on its roof. The German crews were dead and Hinton was prone in the road seemingly oblivious to the fact that he had been shot in the stomach. Taffy was away in the distance chasing more Germans in the darkness.

Sergeant Hinton won a Victoria Cross, presented to him in a POW Camp. None could have been more deserved, but as far as I know Taffy, whose name I never discovered, got nothing.

On my own once again, I thought I would go back to the cellar to find John and the others. I passed a badly injured German officer lying by his defunct gun and gave him some cigarettes. The cellar was empty but a little further on I came across a dozen or so German prisoners being led away with their hands up. Among them was Otto. I took them over and headed for the beach. Otto was nervous; he obviously thought that I had shot his sentry earlier and that he was likely to be similarly treated. I told him that if the Navy came he would be taken to Egypt and treated well as a POW. I would, I said, take him out to dinner.

On the beach I gave up my prisoners to the New Zealanders, and tried without success to find the remnants of my Regiment. I wandered back into the town and fell in with a New Zealander carrying a Bren gun. We had barely introduced ourselves when we heard the now familiar pop, pop, popping of a German motorcycle combination. We rushed into the nearest house and took up position at a first floor window. More Germans appeared, a target too good to miss. I grabbed the gun and emptied the magazine. At that moment, the last few weeks and months overwhelmed me. Night after night, bomb after bomb, no regiment left, Cecilia and the baby, no mail, a fuck-up on the beaches, Billy gone and me here, with a Bren gun, and out there the enemy. The New Zealander went out to look at the dead and the dying. I did not and remember only how much nicer they looked without their steel helmets which had rolled off as they fell.

We went back to the beach and heard that the Navy would take off only the sick and the wounded, believing that the German Divisions had arrived at the coast in force. We knew better, but there was nothing more to do. I was taken to the Brigade Commander who, knowing that I spoke German, had a job for me. As the Navy had refused to evacuate us he was forced to surrender some 10,000 men at dawn. I was to convey this message to the German Headquarters so that the packed beaches would not be bombed at first light. I was to take my German Officer friend with me as a guide. I told Otto, who addressed his fellow captives before we left. They let out a tremendous cheer, quickly stifled under threats from the infuriated Australians.

Otto and I set off once more. No training manual that either of us had read covered our mission. We decided that I would go first shouting: 'I am a British officer with a German,' on our side of the town, after which he would lead and make similar noises in what we imagined might be the German sector.

We wandered round and round and through the square, the scene of my brainstorm. I told him what I had done. He shrugged. He said it was a pity; they were good men; one had just won an Iron Cross, First Class. I muttered, 'Fuck him' under my breath.

By now the poisonous thorn in my foot, my only wound, had made walking almost impossible and it was with much relief that we eventually found Otto's headquarters. He left me outside and went in. The sentry gave me a cigarette. After about half an hour I was ushered in. It was just like a film set. Around a candle-lit table sat half-a-dozen officers. All got up, saluted me and gave me food and schnapps. I told them of the beaches, the coming surrender and the lack of food and water. I asked them, please, to stop the bombers. They said they would and mentioned that they had lost nearly 75% of their force. I went to sleep on a mattress, still wearing my revolver, for which I had never had any ammunition. 'Loopy,' said Otto, 'tomorrow I shall have to take your pistol away.' And tomorrow they did, but not until after I had motored with the German commander to the Brigadier on the beach and he, faced with no alternative, handed over to captivity 10,000 men.

When soldiers are taken prisoner their first reaction is to blame someone – anyone. Many on that beach blamed the Brigadier. Many more blamed the Navy. Some blamed Wavell, some the Government and some the Greeks. For my part, I blame a combination of circumstances which, once under way, led to an unstoppable chaos. Recrimination is fruitless.

The Germans struck a medal and gave their highest award to *Oberleutenant* Otto Hertzog, who as a prisoner, 'frightened the British High Command into surrendering'.

SIX

Prisoner of War

We were taken to a Greek barracks in the town. There we fell asleep, on the floors of the huts and on the ground, for at least 24 hours, exhausted and sick at heart. During the next few days those whom we had fought against went away and were replaced by guards of a most unpleasant disposition. We were constantly hungry, but my own discomfort was much alleviated by once again meeting up with others of my Regiment. Our fellow sufferers were a varied lot; apart from the British there were Australians and New Zealanders, not too pleased with the mother country for landing them in this predicament, Cypriots who quarrelled a lot among themselves, and most unfortunate of all, a well-disciplined group of Palestinian Jews that some unthinking staff officer had sent on this ill-fated expedition.

Barney Lillingston was appointed Senior British Officer and I became the Camp interpreter. Daily we went to the Commandant's office to complain about the food and the hygiene, and daily we were chased down his steps at revolver-point. Food is rather a grand term to describe the maize mealy-meal on which we had to survive until Greek traders were allowed to sell us some vegetables through the wire. Most of us suffered from a dysentry so bad that we could not reach the latrine trenches and had to squat in the open near our huts, hour after hour. A number died. It would have been relatively easy to escape from that camp if one had been able to keep one's trousers up for long enough.

3. My father at the tables (seated, right, with cigarette).
A cartoon drawn in the 1920's. On his right is Dorothy Paget. On the croupier's left is Thelma Furness. The author would be happy to hear from anyone who can identify any of the others.

4. Eilen Roc, the house at Cap d'Antibes which my father lost in a night at the Casino. Photograph taken in 1989.

5. My mother, myself aged three months,
my brother Lawrence aged three years, 1915.

One day I was sent for to interpret for a distinguished visitor. Keeping my trousers hitched as best I could with my hands in my pockets, I found myself face to face with Himmler and a number of mackintoshed henchmen. I bitterly complained about the food situation and the disease. He replied that it was difficult to move regular supplies in such a disrupted country. I told him that when our positions were reversed, we would look after our prisoners better.

'So Herr Hauptmann, you think you will win the war?'

'Of course, and no doubt soon.'

'So.' And with heavy and cynical emphasis, '*Leben Sie wohl.*' Farewell. And the arch villain put out a hand which I managed to avoid shaking.

On reflection, I believe the starvation to have been part of a systematic weakening process so that our will to escape during the subsequent route march and train journey to Germany would be impaired. We began by marching 30 miles to a railway station, and we must have appeared a sorry lot. One young Officer dived under a truck to escape the sun and was shot dead by the same guard that had shot and wounded another for failing to keep up on the march.

We were bundled on to the train, forty to a cattle truck, the doors shut and a fifth of a loaf of bread and a cup of water a day to sustain us for the long journey through Yugoslavia and Austria to Germany. At a Yugoslav station in the middle of a night, the doors parted and food was thrown in to us by local partisans. There was dysentery still, and more died before we arrived in the Fatherland to be herded by guards who revelled in victories in which they had played no part, and who aroused in us contempt where before, in battle, there had been respect. *Aus* and *raus*, *ab* and *weg*, *schnell* and *tempo*; on and on.

Oflag VI B, for British Officers, was at Warburg, Near Kassel in Westphalia. For the first time we were documented and numbered, a small premium on our peace of mind as that number would go home and 'Missing believed Killed' would become POW. And soon Cecilia would have our baby.

The Camp was full of Dunkirk veterans – Old Kriegies. Not yet recipients of Red Cross parcels, they lived on German rations and occasional goodies sent from home. They gave us all their precious cigarettes, at a time when the most senior of officers would rake the dust for fag-ends: we were thinner than they; our need was greater. It was brought home to me, not for the first time in my short military career, that it doesn't matter what you do, it's who you do it with that counts.

One of our many speculations during prison life was who, among our fellow captives, would write a book about it after the war, and why. Mostly we were right and none, I believe, gave a genuine account of how people behaved in that enforced and artificial environment. We all lived at the lowest common denominator of life; peers and farmers, solicitors and their clerks, soldiers and civilians. A truly communist society, all for one and one for all perhaps? Not a bit of it; despite the selflessness and the boundless generosity, the thrifty saved their food and became capitalists – slaves to the market economy – and others, too weak or too profligate, waited for the strong to help them. Many, perhaps all, were ashamed and many hid that shame by blaming others for their capture. The ubiquitous 'They' loomed large in the many discourses on unfairness and the rotten luck of life. At the beginning most in Warburg were the victims of retreat, even rout, and felt it keenly. Later the balance changed and our ranks filled with fighting men: RAF pilots, commandos and others, taken at the sharp end of war. These men felt differently, never doubting for a moment that they, and others like them, would assure ultimate victory: 'Just an interlude, old man, we'll beat the bastards soon.'

It was the duty of an Officer to escape. The choice was limited: over, under or through the wire. Escape attempts had to be organized: to defeat the Goons one had first to win the approval of the Broons. The latter was that unhappy band of Camp officials, ranging from the Senior British Officer (SBO) to the postman. Foremost among the Broons in this context was Mr X – the Escape Officer. To Mr X had to go each and every escape plan; first for his approval and then to a committee headed by the SBO.

The SBO was Major-General Victor Fortune, bagged at Dunkirk while commanding the Highland Division. He looked every inch the German's dream of a British general and had gained a moral ascendency over the Camp Commandant and all our guards from the moment he arrived. The Commandant, large and blustering, was known to the prisoners as Bulk Issue, and was wont to retreat to stand on his dignity when confronted by the General. He had once complained bitterly that neither he nor his officers were ever saluted in the Camp. The SBO reminded us gently that the Geneva Convention demanded such courtesies and we saluted punctiliously from then on – our salutes invariably being followed by deep and exaggerated bows. In such small ways did we amuse ourselves and ameliorate our frustrations. Life for we lesser beings was a constant battle for the moral ascendency so effortlessly assumed by the SBO.

Room 12, Block 5 contained a full house of 4th Hussars; six double bunks with bed-boards, straw mattresses, rough blankets, one small stove, five stools and a carbide lamp. Twelve men, restless boredom and unvarying routine; broken occasionally by flashes of news gleaned from clandestine radios, provoking well-worn reactions.

Each day begins with *Appel*, the roll-call. We shuffle out, bolshie and shambolic; and while half the Goons try to count us the other half turn the huts over, looking for they know not what, but certain that there is something. Tempers are short and the Germans soon begin to shout, giving rise to ritual roars of 'Quack, quack' from the assembled inmates. *Appel* and searches over, we return to the huts. It is winter so the stove has run out of fuel. Some go back to bed, others read or study, and some await the assembly of the poker school. Yet others look mysterious and disappear with bed-boards to shore up the umpteenth tunnel. Cyanide Sid objects:

'I've only got three boards left. Bugger this escaping business; they got me in here, they can get me out. Bluffy, pass me up my book, will you?'

Bluffy chucks the book and it misses, bringing down Sid's shelf, photographs of home and a carefully preserved crust of bread.

'Silly bugger,' says Sid.

'Sorry,' says Bluffy and goes off on watch duty for Mr X. There's an awful lot of watching with so many tunnels.

'The trouble with Bluffy,' resumes Sid, 'is that he can't read.'

'Oh do shut up,' pleads the Broker. 'I'm trying to study my law. Let's have a quiet day.'

Something in the City before the war, the Broker had Sid as his Squadron Leader in the Regiment and in Greece he had been sent to blow up a bridge. He had radioed back to Sid that a Greek general was standing in the road and was threatening to shoot him if he carried out Sid's orders. Sid had simply replied: 'Goodbye'. The bridge was blown.

Francis and the Boy Wonder are brewing up; Francis a regular soldier and immaculate, the Boy Wonder straight from Captain of Games at Eton. Francis has invented the Little Winner, a personal stove made from a Klim tin. They will be much in use today: the Red Cross parcels are due.

'I've finished my book. Let's go for a walk and find some Goon to bow to. Coming, Dormouse?' This from Flossy, brave, intelligent, kind and next for Bart; almost a caricature of aristocracy. Dormouse is our technician and had attached himself to us in Greece having been separated from his RASC unit. He is the most expert of the forgers.

All is quiet; the Broker resumes his study and the Boy

Wonder considers whether or not he has enough energy to play football this afternoon. Francis gives him his own precious sugar ration for extra energy. The day is going well – even with some speed. There is something to look forward to in the parcels and the mail too is due today. Lunch is soup, water, lentils and a bit of potato peel. This evening there might be a feast. I wonder whether my parcel will have a tin of treacle pudding: treacle pudding and cigarettes are the main camp currency. The afternoon drifts on. The Boy Wonder plays football and the bookie pays out the winning bets in Laager Marks with which toothpaste and razor blades can be bought.

The postman comes and interest stirs. Some have several letters, some, me included, none. I go for a walk, not to bait the Goons, but to look throughtfully at the fence. The parcels arrive, wonderful but no treacle pud for me. I barter some cigarettes for half Bluffy's. The News Broon comes round to tell us that the Russians have captured Omsk. 'Isn't that marvellous?' Those that have letters agree enthusiastically that it is. In the evening the carbide lamp flutters, flares and goes out. There is some light from the Klim tins brewing up the oft-brewed tea-leaves, fuelled by bits of the *Volkische Beobachter*. We climb into bed; the remaining bed-boards creak and there are a few sighs before the nightly prep-school, nonsensical ritual begins:

'Ahoy there, what ship's that?'

'The SS *Crow*.'

'Where are you bound?'

'Buenos boss.'

'What's your cargo?'

'Women and booze.'

'Ha bloody ha.'

'The Mardi Gras.'

Then the snores and the constant dribbling of the pee bucket outside our door. Day after day, month after month, year after year. And we were all grown up and all succeeded in the life after this death.

Put a thousand educated men together, give them nothing and soon they will have a great deal. Not a lot of food, perhaps, but forged passes, copied uniforms, Reichmarks and even radios. All of them aids for aspiring escapers.

Most waking hours were devoted to thoughts of escape. Given the brain-power, the time available and the quality and boredom of the opposition, the mechanics were not difficult. Over, under or through, all had their proponents and attempts were frequent and successful. Getting out was relatively easy; staying out appeared impossible. Six weeks seemed to be the bogey time and then the sheepish return and the spell of solitary in the guardroom cell beyond the wire.

We made our application for a tunnel. Tools were issued and promises of clothing, passes and maps. We dug and dug, or rather, scraped and scraped. Inch by inch, through dirt and damp and dropping the debris of our labours dribble by dribble down the latrines where, not known to us, an even smellier tunnel was in being. Our entrance was under the theatre and unpopular with some, as it heralded retribution in the form of closure should we be discovered. And discovered we were; near completion and we never found out how. Bulk Issue arrived triumphant and I was pulled out by my heels – ours was not a ritzy tunnel and there was no room to turn round! The theatre was closed for a month and we were taken to the Commandant for trial. Our sentence was three weeks' solitary but the privacy of those cells was much sought after and there was a long waiting list. Back we went to the hut to await our turn.

When it came, we were again marched through the gate and ordered to leave our blankets in a pile outside the cells while we were taken in and searched. It occurred to me that, concealed in those unattended blankets, it would be possible to slip away while the guards were inside the guardroom with their charges. I pondered for my three weeks and learnt then that all three of us had been struck by the same thought. Back to Mr X we went and he and the committee were enthusiastic. No one had thought of this before and we were given an early date.

There were two problems: first we were all so weak that carrying a fourth in a blanket might be beyond us; second we would have to engineer a group return to the cells once again. We solved the first by enlisting a huge Australian from next door and the second by refusing to turn out for *Appel*, choosing instead to play Bridge, a game of which our Australian friend had not heard and viewed with some suspicion.

In the event it proved necessary to involve the whole cell intake on that day to huddle round the four of us carrying the moving blanket containing Francis, the smallest member of the hut. We all cast our loads on top of him as we were led in to be searched. It worked like clockwork; the pile grew and the guards remained unsuspicious. Before Francis could move, a new Goon squad appeared and assembled in three ranks close to the blankets. Still they did not see him and about-turned to march off to their posts. Francis bolted and dived head-first into a rain-water butt where he remained until darkness allowed him to slip away. Bang on six weeks he was back, caught at the frontier and badly bitten by a dog.

'Told you so,' said Sid.

Jack Fawcus had been a brilliant jockey before the war and had partnered Golden Miller in his prime. He and I were sent together to the camp hospital outside the wire when we could no longer stand because of dysentry. We were treated as best the Germans could and recovered some of our stength. Some French forced labourers were working in the building and their very brave foreman made available to us a wooden plank. Brave because, if found out, he would have been shot whilst we would merely have been returned to the cells. We planned to run the plank from our window across to the perimeter wire of the hospital compound and then jump. It all seemed very simple and as long as we timed the moving searchlight's beam right we should get clear away. Things went well; the sentry seemed deaf to the thumps as we hit the ground and off we scuttled into the heady exhilaration of freedom.

Our next plan was simple too: we would walk westward until we hit the sea and then row until we landed at home. We walked only at night in the approved fashion and not being under the benevolent auspices of Mr X, we had only a rudimentary map and a pin compass. By day we slept and Jack would insist on doing so with a framed photograph of his wife by his head. I was terrified lest the sun catch it and glint our position away.

We stole our food. I had learnt burglary in my idiot days before the war. One night Billy and I, returning to Aldershot after some beano, argued about how easy it would be. To prove the point we stopped at random and burgled the nearest house. The dining-room was full of cups won at golf and we took them. To ease our consciences, we also burgled the house next door and left our booty there. It wasn't quite so easy in Germany where every house had its dog.

One night, crossing a railway line on a road, I tripped and fell over the barrier. A sentry shouted 'Halt' and I fled one way and Jack the other. They opened fire but in the dark had little chance of hitting us; the difficulty was that Jack had the map and I the food. We each went on alone and, being alone in Holland, it seemed sensible to seek the help of a priest. He gave me a bed but would offer no more. The Germans, he said, would take reprisals against the village if I was discovered. I slept, to be woken by a *Wehrmacht* officer and a shame-faced priest. I was taken twenty miles to gaol to find Jack in the next cell. Our six weeks were up!

Our new gaoler was a most menacing-looking Dutchman with a shaven bullet head. As soon as the German Officer left with a promise of an early return, he came clanking down to the cells and beckoned us out. Jack and I looked at each other uneasily but he led us to his house which adjoined the lock-up, and fed us from his own few rations, telling us how he and his wife hated the Nazis.

Once back in our cells, we were collected by a flattering escort of six parachutists and taken over the border to Germany for questioning in a dungeon cellar with no light, ventilation or loo. We were brought food by a blond blueprint of an SS officer who promised us that we would be shot in the morning. What seemed more important to us at the time was the need to find a place in our cell where we could excrete without spoiling the floor on which we slept. In the morning we were not shot; instead we were bundled on to the back of a lorry to begin the long trip back to Eichstatt.

The Camp was now overflowing with the survivors of Dieppe – mainly Canadians – battle-hardened and bursting to escape. Football was largely replaced by softball and the Boy Wonder was much enthused. Indoors, poker took over from bridge as the fashionable game in order to satisfy the growing mania for gambling. Losses were huge and the currency was often in promises of Sterling.

The Canadians were in particularly bad odour with their captors for some ass had left a copy of their operation orders on the Dieppe beach, in which it said that all prisoners were to be handcuffed. Some had been found, not only handcuffed but dead.

One day I was the holder of a particularly good hand of poker when the call for *Appel* came at a most unusual time.

'What the hell do they want now?' asked John.

'I bet it's the RAF again,' said Sid. 'Another bloody useless tunnel.'

'*Aus, aus, schnell*,' said a Goon, tipping my winning hand on to the floor.

'They're going to shoot us,' said Bluffy, quite happily, 'Look . . .'

Machine guns were being brought into the camp, and set up.

'Ha bloody ha,' said someone, 'What about the Geneva Convention?'

'Mind my photographs,' protested the Broker as a guard turfed him off his bunk, 'Bloody Kraut.'

'*Raus*,' said the Kraut, '*Raus*.'

'Quack,' we said, 'Quack, quack.'

The Commandant and his staff were standing behind the guns; he started to speak, or rather to shout. German prisoners, he bawled, had been found on the beaches of Dieppe wearing handcuffs. In view of this the German High Command had ordered that 200 allied prisoners should be handcuffed forthwith. The gates opened and in marched 200 pairs of handcuffs borne by an equal number of guards. There was a silence and then a volume of laughter that I have never heard equalled. It redoubled as those latest on to the parade were shackled. We howled with mirth and the Germans retired bemused. They had been prepared for a full-scale riot and had no idea how to deal with such hilarity. Shamefaced, they withdrew the machine guns. Someone soon made a key and then many more; the handcuffs went on and off as we pleased. For the representatives of the Swiss Red Cross they went on, accompanied by cowed looks and accusations of barbarity. In that childish world of tit-for-tat the allied authorities, when they heard of our treatment, handcuffed German prisoners to match. They got, not laughter, but violence.

As the war came closer, Americans began to arrive and at first they were hard to like. It seemed that they had taken on the enemy single-handed: 'Leave it to us, Mac'. Each had an interminable hard-luck story and insisted on telling it. Soon we stopped listening and, deprived of an audience, they kept themselves apart. Slowly, as the bullshit faded, the thaw came. They played cricket with us and we played baseball with them. They joined in our poker games and shared our

Red Cross parcels. When the Germans shuffled them off to a camp of their own, they sang Auld Lang Syne and we waved them good-bye with genuine sadness.

Oberleutnant Otto Hertzog was true to his word. He had sought me out and, covered in decorations, had obtained permission to take me out to lunch. Keen as I was to have a proper meal and see the outside world again, my feelings towards the Germans had now reached a point where even old friends could not heal the wounds. I had decided not to go until persuaded to do so by the SBO, who thought that interesting information might come my way.

Otto, now with only one arm, was solicitous and asked me how we had been treated in Greece. I told him that we had been treated well by our captors but abominably later by the second-line troops. He reminded me that he had feared such a thing and changed the subject confidently to our conditions in Germany itself. No doubt, he asserted, we were being treated correctly now. I felt that we were talking at cross-purposes:

'Look, Otto, I weigh 9 stone. Less. I was 12. If it were not for the Red Cross parcels I and many like me would be dead.'

'Dead?'

'Yes dead; of starvation. When we finish this nice meal we will go back past the Russian Camp. Hardly any of them have the strength even to walk.'

'I have not seen a Russian Camp here in Germany, but I have seen some for your British soldiers. They are the best advertisement for England. They are all so smart and well-disciplined and clean.'

With that I could agree. I had seen a working party of British soldiers on the way to lunch. They were sitting down and exhorting the Goons to do their digging for them in exchange for cigarettes. The Goons dug.

We ate our food and it made me feel sick. We drove back past the Russian camp and that made Otto feel sick.

'But Loopy, you do not know how the Russians treat our

soldiers. I lost this arm at Stalingrad. In a counter-attack I came back to some of my own troops taken a few hours before. They were motor-cycle troops. You remember motor-cycles, Loopy? We found twenty of them; they had been murdered and castrated. Their genitals had been stuffed into their mouths.'

We didn't talk much more after that and when we reached the Camp Otto gave the Commandant the Nazi salute; to me he gave the old German army version. He held out his hand and I shook it; he was to return to the Eastern Front the next day and he did not come back. I had no interesting information for the SBO.

Shortly after this unusual interlude in a prisoner's life, I and a few others were moved to a camp at Rothenburg, well to the south. This was meant to be a camp for naughty boys but was, in truth, probably a little more comfortable than Eichstätt – perhaps because the Germans could now sense the end of the war. As the allied lines came nearer, escapes were more successful. Fewer went out but a high proportion of those that did got home. The Germans now had listening devices and would descend on tunnels when they felt the diggers had been harmlessly occupied for long enough; after each such operation there would be a camp search. Sometimes this was done by the Gestapo who, not wise in the ways of POWs, would discard their coats as they toiled and could rarely find them again. Towards the end we had so many coats that we began to give them back. We were now winning more than one war.

New guards arrived to take the place of those fit enough to fight: old men and boys, the latter often vicious and keen to destroy our personal possessions. We would walk the camp now, not to bait these pathetic and unpredictable Goons, but to admire the American bombers, nose to tail in full daylight.

'Home by Christmas,' said Bluffy minutes before we were given orders that we were to be moved deeper into the Reich.

'Told you so,' said Sid.

I had had enough; enough of moving; enough of prison; enough of everything except food and mail. I determined that I wasn't going very far this time and neither was Humphrey Luya, a new-found friend from the Royal Artillery. He and I would stick together and, at the first opportunity, bolt. As the long, weary column marched up a hill beside a wood, we broke ranks and fled. There was a fusillade of shots and then a blessed silence; there was too much guarding of the column to be done to spare anyone to chase us. We ran on and then lay still as it became apparent that we had arrived in the middle of a German position. For two days and nights we remained in our thicket. Only one could sleep at a time as we both snored. Only one went for a drink at the nearby stream and we had but one tin of condensed milk between us. After forty-eight hours the Germans left and we made our way to a road. On it and unattended stood a Mercedes staff car. We got in and drove off round a bend – to be saluted by a German Corporal and his section.

Round another bend there was a tank and on the tank was a single white star. The Americans didn't shoot at us, just told us to stop. We got out, filthy in battledresses that had been lying in the mud and rain. We told them who we were and they said they had just passed by the camp. They suggested that we might like to get our own back and invited us to jump on the back of a tank. 'Not bloody likely,' we said, 'we're going home.'

The Americans told us to motor on to the town nearby, where they said we would find their Headquarters; there we would be fed and clothed. For the first time we realized how free we were. Hum accepted a cigar.

There had been a little fighting in and around the town and in the camp I found that a shell had gone through my bed. Out of his house came the Commandant: 'Ach Hauptmann Kennard, I see that you have escaped. I am so glad. The

Americans have let the Russians out and I am nervous for the safety of my daughter. Can you arrange a guard for me?' 'Go to hell,' I said. 'Bloody sod,' said Hum. The Russians could be seen in a field, weakly and vainly trying to catch some sheep for food.

The Americans piled our car high with rations and petrol and asked us to go to the town-hall to supervise the handing in of arms and cameras. We felt we should help and watched as the obedient Germans queued to do as they were told – as they always have done. This chore completed, and with six liberated Leicas in the car, we continued west, seeing very few soldiers of either side until we ran across more Americans. They tried to give us food but there was little room and we were already feeling sick. They had just captured an SS officer who had been told to show them how a German bazooka worked. He was bent over the gun, bemused and desperate, as the Americans shouted at him. Then they told him to walk, then run, and then they shot him.

'I bet the prisoners in allied hands have a lovely time,' Bluffy was wont to say. Sid would have said: 'Told you so.'

We drove on, breaking into empty German houses at night and sleeping in clean sheets. Passing Americans refuelled us and ferried us across rivers where the bridges had been blown. And so we got to Paris and found taps out of which came hot water. We gazed in wonder at this miracle and asked if we could telephone home. That was not possible but they put us on a plane to England – and another camp. We asked if we could telephone home. That was not possible so we made our last escape. I to her.

SEVEN

Soldiering On

The British Army used to publish a manual called *Administration and Morale*. In trying to cover all aspects of both these important subjects one of its editions, published soon after the war, pronounced that the greatest single factor affecting the morale of armies was women. It then went on to add, in less than measured tones, that the behaviour of wives during the recent conflict was often bad enough to cause great concern.

It was certainly true that there was much and deep unhappiness in the enforced separations and unsettled futures which wartime brought. Widespread evidence of this was apparent from the censoring duties which I and most other Officers had to undertake. The misery experienced by fighting men was not so much born out of the fear of death or the pain of wounds but from the loneliness engendered by being apart from loved ones, and the absence of regular letters.

At home young women, often marrying in a hurry to gain the illusion of security, would conceive and were then left alone to struggle with pregnancy, birth and childhood. England at war was a dark and cheerless place with blackout and queues. Who could blame those still young and blooming for finding comfort, however fleeting, in another's arms? Most, of course, did not break the faith and bore the hardships and their drabness with steadfast fortitude, whilst growing older and more careworn.

In Warburg some had many letters in the prison post; others did not and I was one. Some who had many letters found unhappiness on their return. I did not.

Cecilia and I met in London. After four years I said, 'Umm' and she said, 'Er'. I was staggered by her beauty standing now so close before me. She, in her turn, was bewildered at my gauntness. She said:

'Darling I'm sorry, I have the curse.'

And I said: 'Darling I'm sorry I'm so very thin.'

Gently she nursed me back and we went home to Thorpe and our daughter. In Paris I had swopped the last of the Leicas for a teddy-bear; I gave it to Zandra whom I saw now for the first time, and she bit me hard. I shouted, 'Bugger' as I always had in prison when taken by unpleasant surprise. There we stayed for weeks and weeks in Northamptonshire, in England, where things grew and I was free and happy.

Flanked by its village, Thorpe has stood in stone grandeur for a time longer than memory of Shakespeare. On the walls of the great hall hang suits of Cromwellian armour, once worn by the ancestors of those who still live there. Here Cecilia was born and Zandra too. The Maunsels lived there then, Cecilia's much respected parents, who sat year after year in the dining room, the highly polished table keeping them some forty feet apart: Cokayne the squire, JP and fanatical about his partridges, and Eileen, orphaned in her childhood and brought up by an impoverished peer-guardian in some comfort but much neglect. They communicated with each other only sporadically when meeting daily at lunch, and sometimes after supper in the library where Cokayne was at his happiest with his books.

They were, in their separate ways, very kind to me and I was always asked to shoot the partridges and picnic with his friends in the yard; we were not allowed in the dining-room on shooting days for Eileen had a monumental fear that someone 'would bring dirt into the house'. In this lonely and extraordinary way Cecilia was brought up. There were governesses galore – mostly vile – and she was not allowed to dilute her loneliness with dog or cat, because such things, of course, would 'bring in dirt'. The many stables were spotless but empty as Cokayne did not hunt; Cecilia's friends were the frogs in the pond who returned faithfully each spring to spawn; but frogs are hard to tame. So in solitary she grew up, to be launched into the social world by a cousin in London who knew about such things. There was much to see and sample and learn beyond anything that she had dreamt; Thorpe, the silent house, was not versed in the ways of the world.

Within this cocoon I was getting fatter and fitter. England was tired, its rations short and its queues long, but I found it heaven just to go and buy a bun. The harvest was in and the duck would come out of the sunset into the corn behind Tom Hales' stooks. Tom was the farm foreman as had been his father and grandfather before him. Never once in his fifty years had he left the land that bore and now sustained him. He believed neither in holidays nor fertilizers. Weeds were, to him, nature's medicines and there were constant battles with the gardeners on this and other accounts.

Cubhunting began and Cecilia and I were lent horses and shared our fun. Autumn stretched into winter and still there were no orders for me to return to military duty. We planned the hunting season together and I bought a coat. 'What hunt?' the tailor asked. 'The Pytchley,' I replied, and soon a magnificent pink affair with a white collar arrived. If there is a heaven on earth, this was it; the hounds were fast, our horses fit. We were in love; life was splendid and I was in my beautiful new coat. I had not been brought up on the hunting field and it never occurred to me that my distinctive white collar, of which I was so proud, was an award in the gift of the Master. One day they gently told me as they picked me out of a ditch, and that same day the Master honoured me.

We lived in a void where time seemed not to exist until, at last, the world caught up with us. Mama died in the bottomless misery of her Home and I thought that I should take

Cecilia to France to see my father. Apart from a brief dart to Paris during her Season, she had not been abroad, and our journey was not what I would have chosen for her – we took it in turns to share a loo seat on the train from Paris to Nice. Coleridge was living in a cottage, all that remained to him of that beautiful coast; the sun shone and flowers crept in at the windows. The Villa Mary Graham was a ruin; three military occupations in quick succession had stripped it to dereliction. My father, too, was derelict, back once again on his wretched dope. 'He's been very naughty,' said his nurse. The coast was now a leave centre for American troops, who more than deserved their fun, but it was not for me and we left sadly for home.

In England I found Lawrence, now demobilized and settling down again to his beloved racing although his red-head bride had galloped through his capital while he had been away. When I had left for Africa with Wavell, Lawrence had just been demoted from Lance Corporal; later he became a Major in the Intelligence Corps where he had done excellent work and had been badly wounded. He complained bitterly that he, who had not wanted to be a soldier, had collected a bullet in his tummy, another in his knee and an ill-fitting demob suit, whilst I, the volunteer, had had a comfortable holiday for years and was now promoted!

There was news for me from the Regiment. It was stationed north of Klagenfurt near the Wörthersee in Austria, where it was happily engaged in hunting, very successfully, escaped Nazi war criminals, and building up the regimental stable. It was soon to move on to Trieste and would I like to join it there? To begin with there would be no families but it was thought that married quarters would be available quite soon and, oh yes, I was to bring a pack of foxhounds with me.

I claim to love foxhunting as much as any man but I have often felt that the only part of that wonderful sport that can ruin a day is the pack of hounds. A splendid horse, fine fields of grass, laid hedges, a sporting fox and the blood up, all wonderful; and then those damn dogs go the wrong way.

Thanks to the generosity of hunts all over the British Isles: the Woodland Pytchley, the Beaufort, the Galway Blazers, North Northumberland and the Bicester, telegrams began to arrive at Thorpe with news of hounds arriving soon by train. Seven couple were assembled and a most secret rendevous arranged with a Wellington bomber at an airfield in the south of England. I managed to borrow an old and fortunately capacious Austin motor-car, less valuable than its tank of petrol, and set off into the night – apart once again from my family, but with high hopes of seeing them before too long.

Hounds were far from car-trained and I stopped, exhausted, at round about midnight in Regent's Park to give them a walk and myself a rest. Docile somehow slipped away and the last I saw of him was legging it in full cry across the grass. I had a horn but no hound could understand my strangled attempts; I manoeuvered my way back into the car and headed for the airfield. Waiting for me was a very sporting crew, one of whom got bitten and two of whom only narrowly escaped a later court martial. We bundled our fractious cargo on board and headed for Rome. Per Ardua ad Astra may be the motto of the Royal Air Force but it far from suits foxhounds: they set up a howling which never let up, and whilst occasionally drawing breath they chewed on some interesting looking wires through which the harassed pilot was trying to control his aircraft. Seconds after landing the whole RAF crew bolted for the nearest bar leaving me to unload. Dormant was the first to disembark and shot across the tarmac towards one of the seven hills. I set off in pursuit, pausing now and then to blow the horn, but with as little success as in London. I never saw him again.

I now met the familiar administrative hitch, without which the Army would not be half so loveable as it is – the transport sent to meet me had broken down and I was forced to spend my first few hours in the eternal city looking after the remaining six couple of over-excited hounds and trying to answer the obviously puzzled questions of interested Italian airport workers. We got to Trieste eventually and it was difficult to decide whether the enthusiastic reception we received was for me or the animals.

The Regiment was sitting on a political bombshell known as the Morgan Line – a boundary drawn to keep Italians and Yugoslavs apart. The two nationalities hated one another and both disliked the notion of the Line which prevented them getting at each other's throats. Such considerations were, however, matters of complete indifference to the many foxes found in Italy, to the hounds which enthusiastically followed them and to the hundreds of largely unskilled horsemen on liberated horses. Some could barely ride but all were exuberant. Not so the Yugoslavs; they assessed, not unreasonably, that they were being constantly invaded by some sort of irregular cavalry and opened fire. So disturbing did these incidents become to our political masters, that the Commander of 13 Corps, Sir John Harding, who had himself often been out with us and, indeed, fallen over the frontier wall, was forced to order that we stopped chasing foxes with little sense of direction and confine ourselves instead to hunting a drag line. This was a particular pity because some of the more enlightened Yugoslavs had just begun to grasp the idea and had started to come out with us.

Our Headquarters was at Opicina, a village overlooking the Bay of Trieste. The Yugoslavs had occupied it towards the end of the war but it was now to be returned to Italy. The mainly Italian population was delighted with our presence and there were few of the ravages of war that one was to see later in Germany, or indeed which one had experienced in England.

The soldiers loved it. On Mondays the Yugoslavs would march through the town proclaiming death to all Italians. On Tuesdays the Italians would reciprocate with interest and for the rest of the week the gentlemen troopers of the 4th Hussars would take their ease, mostly with an Italian girl on each arm.

A parliamentary commission came out to enquire into the alleged partiality of the occupying British for the Italians in Trieste. We could have saved them the trouble: the fact was that Italian ladies far outnumbered their Serbo-Croat counterparts. The visit was not trouble-free: one MP who had lost his pass was arrested and clapped unceremoniously into the regimental guard-room. The keen young soldier then went off duty, having forgotten to make out his report. It was the next morning before the Orderly Officer discovered and released the unhappy parliamentarian.

We were happy in Trieste, and happier still when the families, Cecilia and Zandra among them, came to live in our requisitioned little villas. A holiday spirit prevailed: with coffee, clothes and cigarettes we bartered for the necessities (and the good things) of life, and the Plain of Lombardy lay at our feet. We kept the peace, which was easy, and we kept ourselves busy, which was not quite so easy for a Regiment full of men waiting to be demobilized and pick up again the threads of their disrupted lives.

We set up leave centres where battle-scarred bodies learnt to water-ski and the even braver hurled themselves down the slopes of Cortina on welfare skis – thus filling once again the wards of the military hospitals only lately emptied of the wounded. Many drove liberated cars and went on leave to Venice. They were not all that impressed with canals and gondolas: 'Like travelling a sewer in a hearse,' was how one veteran of the Gothic Line described it.

The Officers, now that they had their hounds, wanted a Hunt Ball and I was sent by the Commanding Officer, Tony Barne, to the South of France to procure champagne. We set off for Monte Carlo: Corporal White and I with four troopers, a jeep and a 15cwt truck. In Milan we found a very impressive Mercedes staff-car which no one seemed to want and it seemed to me that it would make an agreeable present for the Colonel on my return. We added it to the convoy and resumed our journey. In a Monte Carlo fascinated by my travelling companions and grateful for many years of Kennard subsidy, I was able to get the soldiers into the Casino where they were certainly the first, and probably the only, British troopers in uniform to have gambled at those famous tables. The casino, however, had no champagne and anyway, they said, the French government had banned the export of champagne to Italy. They shrugged their shoulders. Shortly after this depressing set-back I met an American Military Police Officer to whom I explained the problem: 'Sure,' he said, 'You want four hundred bottles, you get four hundred bottles. You reckon that'll be enough? Come back tomorrow and be sure to invite me to your party.'

He was as good as his word, and my little band, with the truck now fairly rattling with the bottles, soon found itself approaching the frontier. As we stopped and the French soldiers, led by a Caporal, approached, I shouted to Corporal White to get my party on parade. I courteously invited the Frenchman to inspect this ad-hoc Guard-of-Honour and he, equally courteously, spat the cigarette from the corner of his mouth, dismissed his men, and accompanied me with a swagger. I suggested that, as the truck was much slower than the Mercedes and the jeep, it could, perhaps, be allowed to go on ahead. He readily agreed. We finished our inspection and he suddenly bawled at his own men to fall in and asked me to do him the honour of returning the compliment. This I was pleased to agree to, after which there was a cursory examination of the two remaining vehicles. We saluted each other and I was then waved on my way.

It was good champagne and, despite Italian roads, some three hundred and eighty bottles made the trip intact. Arrangements for the dance went ahead smoothly until one day I was told that there was an American Captain Goldstein in the Mess; Captain Goldstein wanted payment for four hundred bottles of champagne and he wanted his money in lira, a currency not available to us at that time. All this had been explained to Captain Goldstein who nevertheless appeared to be unhappy; I should take him out to lunch.

I took him to the Fortuna – Trieste's equivalent of the Savoy Grill. He worked his way along the whole line of the bar, trying this and that. At last I got him to a table where he noticed that there was lobster on the menu – at about five pounds a mouthful. He threw the small plate back at them: 'Get me a whole god-damned fish . . .' He ate and drank as prodigiously as any man I had seen, but we settled our problem. We would invite a number of American officers from the neighbouring Blue Devil Division to the Ball and they would pay for tickets in lira. By now he was hardly able to move and he waved me away as he returned unsteadily to the bar, reminding me earnestly not to forget his ticket and to reserve him a Contessa. I complied but he didn't turn up; the Contessa had to be found another partner and, not to be outdone, Corporal White came to the Ball with a Principessa on his arm.

We collected together the necessary lira and tried later to contact Captain Goldstein through his Headquarters. He was not available; there had been one or two irregularities; Captain Goldstein was on his way back to the United States; it probably would be a waste of time trying to contact him again for a year or so. For many years the 4th Hussars had a healthy surplus in the regimental accounts.

Some thirty years later I was telephoned from London by a Mr Goldstein: 'Say, you remember me? And how about that champagne money? No? Well never mind, I'm over here on a visit with the wife and five kids; I'd sure like to see you. We're staying at the Connaught, what about lunch?' My mind floated back to the Fortuna; I shuddered. Not even for a Connaught lunch . . .

The Regiment stayed in Italy for another year, moving twice to carry out a series of post-war occupation tasks, including running a transit camp through which the 1st Armoured Division went home. With little soldiering to keep us occupied, we turned more and more to the horse. There were plenty of them, and many Axis prisoners of war to look after them. We rejuvenated racecourses in Italy by building fences on them and racing under rules. We also took to show-jumping, and in this we achieved an astonishingly high standard.

Seldom in peacetime have I managed to buy a really good horse but the pair I liberated from the Italian Army were wonderful. Hungry, so called because he came from Hungary, won several steeplechases in Italy and Austria under British rules, and Rosso and I were chosen for the British Army Show-Jumping Team.

Post-war show-jumping had already become much bigger business than the amateur competitions at agricultural shows which had been the form in England in the nineteen-thirties. Cecilia and I, together with Corporal Brown, my groom, and Rosso, travelled to competitions in Paris, Geneva, Rome, Berne, Copenhagen and many more. Horses such as Balbo, Notar, Quicksilver and Lucky Find, and soldier-jumpers like Alec Scott, Douglas Stewart and Steven Eve were the precursors of Harry Llewellyn and the golden days of British champions.

Rosso looked like a thoroughbred but it took two men to hold him as I mounted. There was nothing he could not jump and he responded, like a born showman, to the crowds, the bands and the massed banks of flowers at each fence. He was popular with the spectators who, starved of spectacle and colour for so long, flocked to these events. In fact the British teams were generally popular, and wherever we went it seemed that, if their own team couldn't win, it was we who gained their enthusiastic support. Some of the shows pointed up the contrasts to be seen in post-war Europe. In Vienna we jumped in the grounds of the lovely Schönbrunn Palace and the competition was followed by a Grand Ball, the first gaiety the Viennese had organized for many years. Hundreds of people waltzed through the night; jewels, glass and uniforms glittered. But there were no carriages at dawn, just the rubble, the deprivation and the grim patrolling Russian soldiers.

In Berne I met again Frau von Mitzlaff, dearest Mutte of long ago; she was living in Geneva with her sister, Madame de Saugy.

'How are things at home?' I asked her.

'Ah, they have not been good. Those dreadful Nazis . . .'

'But Mutte, you used to love your Adolf.'

'Love him! How could I love him? My home is gone, I have lost my Hubi. Everything is lost.'

She told me that Sven had been badly wounded on the Russian front and Hubi killed over England. The estates, now deep in the Russian zone, had been taken over by the Communists and Daisy and Moni worked on the land there. During the war the Gestapo had arrived to search the house and countryside, pouncing on a suitcase left years before in the attic and engraved with the von Stauffenberg initials. It was 21 July, 1944, the day after the bomb attempt on Hitler's life.

In the early spring of 1947 the Regiment left the sunshine of Italy for the cold winds of the Baltic coast. We had been sent to garrison the Hanseatic port of Lübeck.

We were able to take our families and, of course, the hounds came too. Typically, they howled every inch of the way and there was much to howl about in that devastated land. Lübeck itself, though, had escaped the worst of the bombing and was not laid waste in the manner of Hamburg and the Rühr. The inhabitants were friendly, and in spite of the fatuous no fraternisation rules we all got along well together, happily sharing with the population what we could spare of our rations, and receiving much good-will in return. Our duties were largely those of 'showing the flag', although occasionally something of greater interest came our way. For instance we were asked to provide a young officer to escort Field-Marshal Kesselring from one prison to another whilst the allies wrangled as to whether he should stand trial as a war criminal. (The Regiment, which had fought its way grimly up Italy whilst being opposed by the Field-Marshal's armies, was delighted when it was eventually decided that he was not to stand trial.) We sent a charming Jewish officer who, as the air thawed in the back of the staff-car, was soon exchanging photographs with the old man: 'That is my wife; ach she is an ambitious woman. When I had been a Field-Marshal for three years she told me: "Albert you will never get anywhere, you do not push yourself enough".'

Since we were seldom asked to perform onerous military tasks, we turned our attention once again to hunting. The hounds had been built up into quite a sensibly sized pack and there were still plenty of horses about. We called a Meet and advertised it far and wide within the British Army of the Rhine. We chose a spot central to all: a likely wood, near an autobahn and close to a ramp on which to unload the horses from the versatile Army 3-ton lorries. Several hundred people turned up. Never was there a larger field, nor a more enthusiastic one, and hounds soon caught the spirit of the day as they were put into that wood full of half-remembered scents. Out came hordes of astounded red, fallow and roe deer. Out came angry wild boar, soon to be joined by bemused hares from the fields. We hadn't paid much money, but we certainly took our choice, as we galloped happily after our preferred quarry and a slice of the now hoplessly fragmented pack of hounds. Eventually the whole lunatic day came to an end and we went slowly home. It was left to the co-operative German police to recover all the hounds and return them to kennels. I often think that when the German Government achieved its post-war independence and banned all hunting of live animals with dogs, it did so at the instigation of the police force of Lower Saxony; for too long had they whipped-in to the 4th Hussars' Foxhounds!

The last public appearance of the hounds was in the Olympic Stadium in Berlin, where we had been summoned to take part in a Tattoo, the first of a line of such events which extends to this day. Our part was to present an English village tableau and then hunt round that immense stadium, the scene of many of Lieber Adolf's triumphs – as well as his humiliation by Jesse Owens in 1936.

True to form, the hounds travelled badly and Hannibal bit a Russian soldier at the Checkpoint. This had the not unwelcome sequel that we were waved through the remainder of the formalities without delay. The stadium was as magnificent as I remembered it. Untouched by bombing or the Russian invasion, it was packed each night by a population starved of entertainment and yearning for an extravaganza. Our small scene took place immediately before the final torchlight procession and the massed bands crashing their way through Abide with Me. Invariably the solemnity of this rousing climax was broken by the hounds lifting their legs on everything in sight.

Back at Lübeck the demobilization of our war-time comrades was nearly complete and we were being run down in strength to a cadre of not many more than two hundred. Those of us left were very happy to hear that, seven years after sailing for Egypt, the 4th Hussars were going home.

From home I cashed in on Sir Coleridge's patronage and sent, at M. André's request, the Regimental band to Deauville. *L'orchestre du Regiment de Winston Churchill, le Quatrième Hussar* was a roaring success before the super rich at the gala nights in the Casino. Bandsman Osborne, in his smart blues, gazed wistfully at the expensive bodies on the beach when a bather congratulated him on his smartness. 'More than you bloody well are,' said Bandsman Osborne to the Air Minister of the day. His retort was relayed back to Winston.

The Commanding Officer now was Lieutenant-Colonel George Kidston-Montgomerie of Southannon. He had commanded four cavalry regiments in all and Field-Marshal Montgomery had once described him as the finest commander of an armoured regiment in the Eighth Army. Known to all ranks as 'Colonel George' he was loved, really loved, by everyone in the Regiment. Eton, Oxford and listing his recreations in *Who's Who* as hunting, shooting and fishing, he would be an easy target today for the satirists and the politically superficial. A rich man, complete with silver spoon, he and others like him will be remembered not for their playing fields at Eton but by the men they led and by the war memorials that bear so many of their names. As a leader he was among the finest any of us had known; he had the priceless art of always being where he was most needed, and demanded of others only that which he was willing to try himself. He had great compassion and high good humour; in short he was the ideal war-time cavalry Officer.

George led us back to Colchester where we were met by the news that we were to be drafted to Malaya where, it appeared, there was a little trouble brewing in the way of communist terrorism. Hastily we made arrangements for the housing and welfare of the families as Malaya was accounted, at least at first, too dangerous for wives and children, and prepared ourselves to receive a welcome draft of over four hundred regular soldiers to bring us up again to war strength.

EIGHT

From Active Service To Command

The nine months at Colchester were spent mainly in converting our skills from those required in tanks to those of armoured cars, and in integrating our new manpower drafts into the regimental family. On 20 August, 1948, we sailed from Southampton on the troop-ship *Dilwara*. Colonel George had flown out to Singapore with a small advance party and I was appointed Officer Commanding the troops on board, a not too onerous job largely taken up with organizing daily sessions of physical training (not my cup of tea), and seeing that the favours of the four pretty nursing sisters on board were fairly distributed among the Officers. We had shore leave at Aden and Colombo and were met at Singapore by the Commander-in-Chief, Far East Land Forces, and the Colonel. We marched off to a transit camp where we learnt that George had arranged for a tailor to meet the Officers; we were to be dressed for the forthcoming campaign, not in the uniform laid down in Dress Regulations but in one of a Kidston-Montgomerie design. It turned out to be very smart, a long deep-cut jacket with sloping pockets and trousers of Bedford cord – and exceedingly expensive. It was, of course not to be worn in the jungle, just in our armoured cars, and it often proved the point so dear to George's heart, that scruffiness is not a prerequisite of military efficiency, even on active service.

It was the first time that a cavalry regiment had been seen in Singapore and so, as a climax to our ten-day period of acclimatization, we were to march through the city behind the

Band. That the Band was with us was the direct result of an intervention by Winston Churchill, then leader of His Majesty's Opposition and Honorary Colonel of the 4th Hussars. In Colchester George had had a letter from a Staff Officer in the War Office saying curtly that the Band would not be accompanying the Regiment on its forthcoming tour of active service. George had telephoned Winston who had immediately penned one of his now famous 'Pray tell me' memos: 'Pray tell me,' he had written to the Chief of the Imperial General Staff, 'who has directed that my Band should not accompany my Regiment to Malaya?' A very short time later the order was rescinded.

The ceremonial over, the Regiment deployed far and wide in Malaya. I had the honour to command A Squadron based at Ipoh in the state of Perak; other bases were at Taiping, Kuantan, Kuala Lumpur and Raub. We also had one squadron in Hong Kong where it provided a welcome base for leave away from the threat of terrorism. Our main task was to keep the roads and tracks open by constant patrolling in armoured cars and with dismounted forays into the jungle of up to half an hour's march; operations deeper into the jungle were normally the responsibility of the infantry. Other duties included train guards, escorts for VIPs, occasional deeper jungle patrols and maintaining close liaison with the police and the planters. We had to learn quickly and sometimes painfully. The first A Squadron casualty was the squadron clerk who disturbed a hornets' nest and nearly died from the effects of the frenzied insects' retaliation. Then a young Troop Leader, hot on the trail of a suspected terrorist, saw the fugitive disappear into a hole in the ground and poked his own head in to invite the bandit to surrender. He was shot and wounded, fortunately not mortally. The Squadron Leader had a lot to learn too. I thought it a good idea to test the alertness of one of my outposts by firing a few shots over their heads. I was gratified by their prompt response and alarmed by their accuracy; I never tried that particular ploy again.

The Regiment had been in Malaya only a few months when a Troop led by Lieutenant Michael Questier was ambushed just north of Ipoh; Michael and six soldiers were killed in the subsequent fire-fight. A newly arrived young officer, fresh from Mons, had been sent out with the Troop to gain experience and now found himself in charge. So effectively and with such gallantry did he conduct himself that the bandits were driven off leaving six dead. For this, the officer, Jon Sutro, was awarded the MC and Lance-Corporal Smith the DCM. Smith was one of those soldiers, so beloved of RSMs, whose rank fluctuated like a yo-yo. Soon after his bravery award he was reduced once again to the rank of Trooper for pointing out to the Squadron Sergeant Major, who had himself won a DCM in Italy and was at that moment engaged in trying to close the Naafi bar where Smith and his friends were engaged in a lengthy celebration, that there were now two men of distinction in A Squadron who were clearly equal in all respects.

My few months in the Far East passed quickly. I loved the country, the soldiering and the success we were undoubtedly having, but in France Coleridge had died and at Thorpe Cecilia and Zandra waited. I was not too disappointed to hear that I had been posted as Second-in-Command to the Shropshire Yeomanry.

In 1947 the War Office had had one of its rather rare Good Ideas. Each regular cavalry regiment was to be affiliated to a yeomanry regiment of the Territorial Army. It was our splendid luck to have drawn the Shropshire Yeomanry, which meant, among other things, that we provided that Regiment with a Second-in-Command, an Adjutant and several Warrant and Non-Commissioned Officers as Permanent Staff Instructors skilled in the teaching of the techniques required of tank crewmen.

The Headquarters was in Shrewsbury and I set up my weekly shop at the Red Lion Hotel. Cecilia remained at Thorpe, unable to face another upheaval – she had only recently moved out of the army house we had occupied in Colchester. I was able to go to Northamptonshire quite frequently except at week-ends which was when the territorials did most of their soldiering. The Yeomen were remarkable people who, while holding down a full-time job, reached astonishingly high military standards in what was, essentially, their spare time. Most of them in those days had been in the war and in some ways their successors of the 1980s are even more remarkable: few have previous military experience and the demands made on them, both military and technical, have increased dramatically.

The Shropshire Yeomanry was able to trace its existence back to 1795 and was as proud a regiment as any regular counterpart. In war and peace it, and others like it, cultivated a studied amateur approach which belied their steely professionalism. A good example of what had become known as the 'Yeomanry Spirit' concerned a regiment in Italy which had been selected to spearhead a particularly nasty attack on entrenched German positions. Having listened to his orders, the Commanding Officer prepared to leave Divisional Headquarters to brief his men. At the door he turned and said, 'You must remember, General, that we're not really soldiers.' This remark was not well received, delivered as it was a shade loftily, by a man who had been High Sheriff and Deputy Lieutenant of his county as well as being a Master of Foxhounds. There was no need to worry; the regimental plan was faultless and its execution by the Yeomen was prosecuted with such determination, skill and bravery that the Germans were driven out never to return.

My Commanding Officer at Shrewsbury was Lieutenant-Colonel John Kynaston who had won a DSO in the war. He was a conscientious man in every respect save one – he could

6. With my first wife, Cecilia, at our wedding, 1940.

7. As ADC to General Wavell; *left to right*, Brigadier (later General Sir Arthur) Smith, myself, General Wavell.

8. Sir Winston Churchill visits his old Regiment at Höhne. Standing behind him are myself, then commanding the Regiment, and Brigadier Scott-Cockburn.

never find time to compose the Officers' annual confidential reports. These are, of course, crucial to an Officer's career and even then were taken seriously by the ambitious and the more sensitive as well as by the Military Secretary's branch of the War Office. The writing of them is an important part of a Commanding Officer's duties so at the appropriate time of the year I reminded John gently to get down to the task. He told me to do them for him and he would read, approve and sign the results. There was no problem about this; I had just as much contact with his Officers as he did and our judgements on their performances and capabilities had proved to be pretty similar. Soon they were all completed, signed and posted off to District Headquarters. I was about to turn my attention to the next day's pheasant shooting when it occurred to me that my own report had not been among them. I rang the Colonel at his home:

'Write it yourself,' he said.

'Fine, Colonel. But what about signing it? When will you be in? District are already complaining that we're a bit late.'

'You sign it. Forge my signature; you've seen it often enough to know what it looks like.'

This was an opportunity given to few men; I sat down and composed a masterpiece about the paragon of military virtue that was the Second-in-Command of the Shropshire Yeomanry. In the pen-picture section of the report my prose soared to new heights, and I didn't stint myself either in awarding gradings for Tact, Determination, Initiative, Administrative Ability and the other qualities required of the well-rounded Officer. For Military Knowledge I gave myself an E (for Excellent), the top category and awarded very sparingly.

The District Commander, who had to add a little section of his own as the next senior Officer up the reporting chain, was a little surprised when the document appeared on his desk. He picked up his telephone and rang John to discuss it. The latter was at some disadvantage, having not had sight of the matter now apparently at issue and which appeared above his signature. But he had not run a vastly efficient family estate and won a DSO without possessing a capacity for quick thought. He managed to convince the General that, yes indeed, Kennard was a great deal more accomplished than might at first appear. An E for Military Knowledge? Ah yes, well that might have been over-egging it a bit. The upshot was that I was called to see the General in his Headquarters where he courteously explained to me that he and my Commanding Officer had disagreed over their assessments of my military knowledge and that he, the District Commander, proposed to exercise his right to downgrade that section to Very Good. Did I object? I assured him that I did not and he gave me a glass of sherry. I went back to the office and presented John with a bottle of champagne!

My years with the Yeomanry were very happy ones and we were even able to do our bit in training some of the Z Reservists called up as a result of the crisis in Korea. Z Reservists were ex-soldiers with comparatively recent military experience and with a liability to be called up in an emergency. So good was the Shropshire Yeomanry at reminding these, at first, very reluctant heroes of their military skills that a high proportion of them later applied to sign on as regular soldiers.

During my stay in Shrewsbury the 4th Hussars had returned from its successful tour of duty in Malaya and was now stationed at Tidworth in Hampshire. There I rejoined it, again to command A Squadron. As in Malaya, the Regiment was widely dispersed: at Tidworth, Warminster and Castlemartin in Pembrokeshire. The regular soldiers drafted in for service in the Far East were gradually coming to the end of their time and there was an increasing influx of National Service Officers and soldiers. In August, 1953, we gathered ourselves together and moved to Hohne, a British garrison in

West Germany close to the site of the Bergen-Belsen concentration camp; a place where to this day no birds fly and horses are reluctant, sometimes to the point of refusal, to pass too close. Hohne Camp held several regiments but we were lucky to be blessed with the finest Officers' Mess in Germany – a grand old house known as Schloss Bredebeck, with stables, ornamental gardens, a lake stocked with fish and enough land to do a little pig, chicken and duck farming. I didn't know it then but it was in this lovely place that I was to spend the last four years of my military life in happiness and heartbreak.

The Commanding Officer was Lieutenant-Colonel Stephen Eve, an old friend who had also been taken prisoner in Greece, but not before he had won a gallant Military Cross with which he was eventually decorated after the war. Militarily there was now much to do; an endless round of manoeuvres, beginning as the year began, with Troop training and working up, through exercises designed to test the efficiency of the Squadrons and the Regiment, to the huge formation exercises involving whole Divisions and more, which rolled then as they do now across the North German plain. On one such, called Exercise Battle Royal, I had become so exhausted by lack of sleep that I lay down beside my tank to catch up. The Colonel, annoyed at finding one of his Squadron Leaders asleep at a time when instant activity was called for, kicked me into semi-wakefulness. I, thinking that a lesser being had stumbled over me, roared 'F*** off'. To his eternal credit Stephen did just that – and I returned post haste to the battle!

Our leisure time was taken up with horses, skiing (at Bad Harzburg, close to the East German border), shooting duck on the north coast and over the rivers and fishing for the trout with which we stocked Bredebeck's lake. Horse activities were widespread and took in drag-hunting, hunter trials, show-jumping and racing. Racing was increasingly popular and joint Anglo-German meetings were commonplace, both on the flat and over fences. Stephen and I represented BAOR at international show-jumping events (until I broke my collar-bone in Copenhagen) and I managed to win the odd race on a horse called Glad Awakening who carted me to victory in the German Grand Military. Cecilia was happy and Zandra was at school and happy too; I had my horses and I had Duty, the best yellow Labrador in the world; he will certainly meet me wagging his tail when I snuff it. I was with my other family that is the Regiment and I felt that I could not be more content. But then I heard, in 1954, that I was to command the Regiment the next year in succession to Stephen Eve, and at that moment my cup was truly full.

To command one's own Regiment is the pinnacle of any true soldier's ambition. Even if he goes on to more exalted rank, nothing can compare with the almost overwhelming sense of history felt by the Commanding Officer as he becomes, for two or three years, the custodian of hundreds of years of honour and valour, of success and failure, of happiness and grief and, at the same time the writer of a new chapter. I thought then, and I still believe, that the regimental system is the lifeblood of the British Army and the envy of all foreign powers. When, in 1981, Brigadier Shelford Bidwell wrote a letter to *The Times* advocating a computerised approach to defence, I was prompted to send the following riposte:

> *Computerising the Armed Forces*
> Sir – Perhaps Brigadier Shelford Bidwell, in his computerised solution to defence, has forgotten that the greatest factor in war remains morale.
>
> That morale feeds on the tradition of the Regiment, its history, its customs and its uniform so that in many hundred years the thin red line has never been truly broken. Nor will it be if the man behind the gun remains the same.

There are those who maintain to this day that my appointment was the sole evidence of a sense of humour to be shown by the War Office since the war. In any event I was the proudest man alive when, in February, 1955, I sat in the Colonel's chair. It is, of course, a lonely chair. Gone, perforce, are the intimate and irresponsible delights lately enjoyed with the closest of mates, but I did my best to keep the informal atmosphere with which somehow I had always been surrounded. A help in this was my complete inability to remember anyone's proper name. Nicknames, particularly those invented by me, I could manage, and so there were few, if any, Johns, Peters, Kenneths and Michaels; instead there was The Crow and Glub-Glub; the Badger, the Wombat and the Mountain Goat; Ticker Tom, Plop-Plop and the Dipper. They served me well, those names, except on more formal occasions such as Churchill's visit to Hohne when he was surprised to be introduced to five officers all called Tom Williams. None of the officers, though, so much as blinked!

I was blessed in Captain Tilbrook with an outstanding Adjutant who did much to unburden me from the paper-work I hated. He worked harder than most but even he was sometimes rewarded. One day two senior Non-Commissioned Officers were marched before me having been caught poaching fish from a near-by privately owned lake. Having prised out of them the exact location of this stretch of water and ascertained that the owner was away, I gave the miscreants a rocket, dismissed them and took the Adjutant and Second-in-Command out to try our luck.

There were other hazards, too, for those close to me then. I had been informed that the executors of Coleridge's estate had unearthed a red diplomatic box in Paris and as one of the Officers was on leave there I wired him to collect it and bring it to Hohne. It arrived as the Regiment was leaving on one of the year's major exercises and Jittering Charlie (the Second-in-Command), Ticker Tom (the Adjutant) and I were engaged in last-minute preparations. The box looked exciting and as we forced it open I began to think that at last I was to see something substantial in the way of an inheritance – perhaps some jewellery or priceless manuscripts. Instead we found a number of neatly tied bundles, each one labelled Tashkent 1910, Constantinople 1908, Teheran 1909 and so on. They were packets of dope: hashish and opium. Soon a furious argument broke out between Ticker and Charlie as to whether opium was eaten or smoked. To settle it I suggested that each put his theory to practical test – but not too extensively. My caution was well advised; the Adjutant was sick all over his jeep (and his driver) and the venerable and much respected Second-in-Command fell out of his vehicle on the autobahn.

I was occasionally in trouble with 'higher authority'. During an extended and boring lull in another major manoeuvre I sent a wireless vehicle down to the racecourse at Cologne, where a regimental horse was running, so that the Signals Officer could provide us with a commentary. I was unaware that the exercise was, in part, an experimental outing for a newly formed and very secret wireless monitoring unit whose operators were riveted by the conversation on the 4th Hussar radio network. Retribution was swift but the horse won.

I also got into trouble with the Church. At one big service attended by the Chaplain General I had to read the lesson. I rehearsed my part from St Matthew, but, arriving at the lectern, found that our delightful padre had left the Bible open at Ecclesiastes. Not sure whereabouts St Matthew was, I started where it was open and stopped when I came to several unpronounceable names. The Chaplain General's sermon was no longer on net.

On another occasion there was to be a demonstration of much political significance for a visiting foreign notable. The gallant Brigadier was anxious. Did Kennard really understand how important it all was? He looked at his watch; only an hour or so to go; perhaps he might just take a drive, casually of course, past the site of the demonstration and see if everything was ready and properly organized. He called for his driver and they set off on an unobtrusive route; it wouldn't do for the Regiment to feel that it was being spied upon. As his car approached the scene of the proposed action the Brigadier's heart sank. His worst fears had materialized: there, at a time when shining tanks should have been lined up being lovingly polished by their crews, was a fracas with a most unmilitary aspect. Two tanks had clearly and, in the Brigadier's eager view, carelessly collided. And there, if he was not mistaken, right in the middle of it and probably responsible for the whole sorry affair, was the Commanding Officer of the 4th Hussars. He tapped his driver on the shoulder and pointed to the affray:

'Turn up there,' he said, 'and quickly.' The car changed direction, accelerated, and finally stopped in a flurry of German dust. The Brigadier leapt from it as a lion on its prey.

'Who,' he bellowed, 'is the senior officer here?' I looked around.

'You are, Brigadier,' I said.

One of the perks of being commanding officer of a cavalry regiment in the field is that it is thought appropriate for him to have his own loo, erected by the Provost Sergeant and shielded from public gaze by a canvas screen. It is, rather inelegantly, known as a thunderbox, and my own was to lead to yet another unfortunate confrontation with a different Brigadier. I was engaged in deep meditation on this splendid monument to British sensibilities when the Brigadier arrived. The Adjutant greeted him apprehensively.

'Good morning, Brigadier. I'm afraid the Colonel's on his thunderbox.'

'Go and fetch him.' The Adjutant went, and came back empty-handed.

'He won't be a minute, Brigadier. He's only just gone there.'

'Go and bloody-well get him now. I haven't got all day.'

The Brigadier's temper had snapped and his voice carried miles. The Adjutant turned to run and deliver this latest command. He stopped as my voice drifted faintly but audibly on the breeze.

'Tell the Brigadier,' I said, 'that I can only deal with one shit at a time.'

When an Officer joined I used to try and impress upon him that living dangerously was the best preparation for war and that he should strive to engage in pursuits that frequently frightened him. I would suggest that a horse or even a pair of skis were handy and appropriate mediums to carry out my wishes. One young man, who was to die tragically early of cancer some years after he had left the Regiment and made a resounding success of an unconventional second career, took me at my word and had himself towed at sixty miles an hour on skis behind a car. He nearly killed himself then and ran close a second time when a German farmer fired several times at him with a shot-gun when he inadvertantly destroyed the poor man's farmhouse with a tank barrel when executing a poorly judged turn. They were good times indeed.

The writing of my Officers' Confidential Reports proved to be as onerous a task to me as it had been to John Kynaston in Shropshire. It gave me no satisfaction to write: 'This Officer has chosen the wrong career' or 'I have never seen this Officer without his overcoat', but I thought it better to be blunt and to the point. I gained, I think, something of a reputation for the pithy comment when reporting, but not all my masters agreed with my views. One expressed himself so strongly that I invited him to write the reports himself. He declined but he did, of course, have to write mine. This ultimately bore the Army Commander's postscript: 'Loopy by name and Loopy by nature. Nevertheless he commands the finest Regiment in my Corps.' I was well pleased.

The highlight of this period in my life was my association

with the Colonel of the Regiment, Winston Churchill. As a subaltern in the Regiment in the last decade of the nineteenth century, he had served in Aldershot and India with the 4th Hussars before being seconded to the 17th Lancers with whom he charged at the Battle of Omdurman. As a subaltern he was by no means popular; he continually carped at the way the Officers' Mess was run and was wont to remain in the shade, reading or writing his first book whilst the less industrious went pig-sticking in the sun. An entry in the Wager Book of the Officers' Mess of the time reads: 'Colonel X bets Major Y the sum of five pounds that that bounder Churchill will never be a Cabinet Minister.' When I told him of this wager I received a Churchillian grunt, and 'Did he pay?'

Churchill excelled at polo and was a member of the 4th Hussars side that won the Inter-Regimental Tournament of India in 1899, in which he scored the winning goal. 'Polo is the prince of games,' he wrote, 'because it combines all the pleasure of hitting the ball with all the pleasures of riding and horsemanship; and to both these is added that intricate loyal team-work which renders a true combination so vastly superior to the individuals of which it is composed.'

He had become the Honorary Colonel of the Regiment in 1941 and remained so until his death. In 1956 he came to Hohne to stay with his Regiment for two days. We filled his room with Churchillian and Indian memorabilia, and dined with him in the Officers' Mess. After dinner I was proud to be able to say a few words. I began by welcoming the only guest, the British Ambassador, and then:

> We hope, Sir, for just a few hours, to take you back to the start of a career unrivalled by any man. The start was here, when the Regiment was your home. Around you now are many of the same proud trophies that stood before you then. Amongst them is the Cup won

by your winning goal. . . . As ever, on your right sits the President of the Mess Committee, probably at this moment rather a worried man and on your left, that unhappy chair of which you may have memories, reserved for the Orderly Officer.

Tonight you will meet the true aristocracy of men, the senior Non-Commissioned Officers whose constant and selfless loyalty to the Regiment can never be surpassed and to whom your visit means so much more than higher pay and fewer working hours.

The world in whose destiny you have played so large a part has changed vastly since you charged at Omdurman. Yet during your visit I am confident that you will find that much of value remains unchanged. Finally, Sir, I would say on behalf of the Regiment that whatever changes befall us, you will be our Colonel for many hundred years.

Your Excellency, Officers of the Regiment, I give you a toast. To the greatest Hussar of them all – Our Colonel.

In the Sergeants' Mess the great man was visibly moved when confronted by that body of men Kipling called the backbone of the British Army. Winston addressed them:

I was very glad when the Commanding Officer asked me to come here in order that I should have the opportunity of meeting you and seeing you at work and play. I regard myself as highly fortunate.

There is no doubt whatever that the strength of our people derives itself from a steady stream of Non-Commissioned Officers. There are those who command; there are those who play a wider part, or less violent parts than you. But the Non-Commissioned Officers form a core and a nucleus around which the British Army has always been created, or recreated, and can always strike to a real and devastating effect.

I regard it as a great pleasure and privilege to come here tonight. I thank you very much.

The next day he toured the Regiment before the mass of local and military dignitaries claimed him.

During my years of command I had, at his request, frequently visited him in his London flat. He appeared lonely, and liked nothing better than to remember his days of Regimental soldiering. He never bore me malice, though he knew that I had been instrumental in posting the splendid, ebullient Randolph to more suitable activities than soldiering with his father's Regiment.

Had I read Alanbrooke's diaries? 'Yes.' What did I think of them? 'Brilliant,' I replied tentatively. He had extolled Churchill in his preface, and been very critical of him in his book. A Churchill grunt . . . 'D'you know what I called him? My ruddy Governess.' And it had been that relationship that had done so much to win the war.

A few years later he was to die. The world will remember the dignity of his Lying-in-State, the magnificent, sad funeral procession, the journey in a barge past Thames-side cranes saluting the worn-out body on its way to family interment in a country grave at Bladon.

Here, for his last procession, by his request, the coffin was borne by bearers from his own Regiment. Surrounded by his family, the quiet tranquillity of these last rites was suddenly and distinctly broken by a loud tinkle. What the world does not know is that Sir Winston lies there now with Staff-Sergeant Webb's Long Service and Good Conduct medal close to his heart. It had fallen off the Staff-Sergeant's tunic as the coffin was finally lowered to the grave.

In the Army it is taught that each twist and turn of life can be properly evaluated by making an appreciation of the situation: formulating an aim, considering all the factors and the possible courses open and finally selecting the appropriate course to fulfil that aim. There are few problems which cannot be solved in this way and I had a problem:

'Captain Fearfield would like to see you, Colonel.' Ticker Tom ushered Mark into my office.

'Colonel, I want to leave the Army.'

'But Mark, why? You have just passed the exam into the Staff College; you are one of our most promising young Officers. Your future is practically assured. Why?'

'I don't want to take up my vacancy. If I do I wouldn't be able to resign for five years.'

'But why did you bother to work for the Staff College if you don't want to go?'

'Colonel, may I speak to you as a friend?'

'Of course you may, you bloody fool. Take your hat off and sit down. What the hell's the matter?'

'I've fallen in love with Cecilia.'

'Good God.'

How the devil do you appreciate a situation like that? I went home to lunch.

'Darling, a funny thing happened this morning. Mark came to see me. He wants to leave the Army. He says he's in love with you.'

'I'm very much in love with him too. Sorry.'

Love, that nebulous pursuit of soldier, sailor, tinker, tailor.

But come off it; she had given me her loveliness for as much of those seventeen years as my profession had allowed us to live together. She had retained her loveliness and was saddled with a husband frequently frustrated in his duties, while surrounded by attractive and vigorous young men. There had been times in forced separation and the demands of fit youth when I had not been faithful. Love is not love that alters when it alteration finds. Man loves too fast to be his greatest pleasure. To hate is best, he can detest at leisure. Love, hate: two strong emotions to be appreciated in the situation. And in between indifference – a bore for both. A crossing of the point of no return.

I made my plan. Tradition demanded both a posting to Africa for Mark and a course of honorable action for me. I had to attend a War Office conference and contacted a 'specialist' in these matters. A hotel bedroom and the necessary bill eagerly awaited by hungry solicitors. I got a sort of satisfaction for my money but much more, a salvation, from Zandra who had forgiven us both. The conference received little attention. Back to Germany, where the second blow fell:

> No organism can stay the same for ever. If it does, it dies. Change is inevitable. The thing that matters is the British Army as a whole, and not merely the smaller interests of its component parts, however old and honourable those may be.

With those words of bitter common sense, Field-Marshal Templer announced the amalgamation of the 4th Hussars and the 8th Hussars and a number of other amalgamations too, affecting regiments of equal valour and antiquity.

At the annual get-together of the Old Comrades in London, I had to address them; to persuade them not only to lump it but welcome it. To accept a full-stop to the history of the 4th

Hussars and see that the opening chapters of the Queen's Royal Irish Hussars (for this was what the new regiment was to be called) were happy and efficient and as glorious as the past of the 4th and 8th. It was clear that the Old Comrades, whose happiest memories lay under a single badge, would find the transition more difficult than those serving.

The lead must be given by the young and followed by the old; for the young would write the future and it would be similar to the past.

The human problem was that which worried me most. A number of officers and men, aged between 34 and 44, would have to go – be transferred into other regiments or declared compulsorily redundant. And to complicate matters there would be those who would not be able to face starting again in another regiment but would choose instead to leave the service without the benefit of redundancy pay:

> To stay or not to stay? That is the question.
> Whether it is nobler in the mind to suffer
> The whims and fancies of outrageous Sandys,
> Or to take arms against his every plan,
> And, by resigning, end them; to go, to stay?
> No more; and by a form to say we end
> The heartache and the thousand natural shocks
> Next year will bring. Is that the end
> Devoutly to be wished – to leave, to work?
> To work at something new; aye there's the rub.
> For in that other world what work may come,
> When we have taken off this uniform,
> Must give us pause: Gratuities and
> Compensation too – these must have thought;
> For surely they will not occur again.
> The chance that, if we stay, how long before
> A further cut, or cuts, may follow on?
> To go? To stay? To welcome something new?

Or to remain amongst the things we love,
That make us rather bear those ills we have
Than fly to others that we know not of?
Thus sudden change makes cowards of us all;
And thus the native hue of resolution
Is sicklied o'er with the pale cast of thought,
And enterprises of great pith and moment
With this regard their currents turn awry,
And lose the name of action.

I advertised in the personal columns of *The Times* for jobs for those that had, or chose, to go and the response was remarkable. The advertisement, which ran as follows, caused a good deal of comment at the time:

> Commanding Officer of famous Cavalry Regiment, anxious for future of some Officers and senior NCOs who will shortly become redundant on amalgamation, invites offers of employment. Would prospective employers who have prospects for men to whom pride of service and loyalty mean more than higher pay and shorter working hours, apply directly to me? Offers of dead-end jobs not considered; minimum pay for NCOs £600 a year; officers £1000, both with prospects of advancement. Guaranteed satisfaction from personally selected men, or three months' pay returned in full. – Lt-Col Kennard, 4th Hussars, FPO 30.

In February, 1958, eight months before the amalgamation of my beloved Regiment with our greatest friends, the 8th King's Royal Irish Hussars, I handed over my command to George Butler, an officer of the 8th who had been chosen to be the first Commanding Officer of the Queen's Royal Irish

Hussars; it seemed right that he should be given a chance to get to know at least some of the 4th that he was to lead. I remained on the committee charged with the amalgamation procedures and I was there on the eve of the one hundred and fourth anniversary of the charge of the Light Cavalry Brigade at Balaclava, when the 4th and 8th had charged side by side down the valley of death, to see two regiments become one:

> With measured tread the Regiments march
> away,
> And stilled are centuries of history.
> Only to be revitalised today,
> The whole anew in moving mystery.
> That stalwart band men called the Light
> Brigade
> And others from the sands near Alamein,
> Who also on the altar all had laid;
> A splendid host of witnesses unseen.
> With crisp commands, the pageantry complete,
> And ringing cry, 'God Save the Queen',
> They wheel and march, with perfect rhythmic
> beat.
> The trumpets sound, there breaks another
> dawn,
> A thousand glories once again reborn.

It was time to decide what to do. General Hackett, in one of his books, wrote, "From time to time all soldiers consider whether the time has come to try something else: I had once asked a wise old military bird whether he had thought of leaving. 'Look around you,' he said, 'and if there is a bunch of people you would rather be with, go and join them.' I looked around and knew it could never be like this again. I had achieved success by my own reckoning: I had commanded my beloved Regiment and I had, I felt, done my best. Success in the armed forces is measured in ways other than rank. It lies, perhaps more importantly, in satisfaction. Qualities like integrity, personal loyalty, fortitude and self-effacement enrich any group of men in which they are found. In the military life they have a functional importance not commonly found elsewhere. In some armies, rank attracts a veneration entirely absent in our own. The result is an absence of the relaxed atmosphere found in most of the British Army, sometimes carried to the point of urbane insolence by the cavalry and the footguards. It is said that it was a footguard Commanding Officer who, accompanying a visiting General on a tour of inspection of the guardsmen's barrack accommodation, noticed with some curiosity that the distinguished visitor was poking endlessly into dark corners and under beds.

'I suppose you know what I'm looking for?' said the General.

'As a matter of fact, no Sir,' came the reply.

'Cigarette ends.'

'Oh I am sorry, Sir, I had no idea.' He took out a slim, gold cigarette case; 'Here, have one of mine.'"

During my last few days of command I received a letter and a postcard, both of which I treasure. The letter was from Sir Winston Churchill:

at La Pausa,
Roquebrune-Cap Martin,
A.M. 24 January, 1958

My dear Kennard,

Many thanks for your letter. I am glad to hear that Major Butler has been appointed. He sounds a very good choice.

It also gave me pleasure to know of the Regiment's successes.

It is sad that your own command is coming to an end. Please accept my warm thanks for all you have done for the Regiment. I saw myself during my most pleasurable visit to Celle how your influence permeated through your command, and I think that all members of the Regiment owe you a debt of gratitude for the way in which you conducted Regimental affairs in the last phase before amalgamation.

I hope that I shall see you some time when I am back in England.

With all good wishes,

Yours very sincerely,
Winston Churchill

The postcard, which came from Florida, was from Trooper Smith DCM and said: 'Wish you were here, you old bastard; the climate is much better than it was at Bielefeld'. Bielefeld was the name of the Military Prison in Germany.

The final interview I had with a soldier opting out of the Army was with one Corporal Mabbutt.

'Well, Corporal Mabbutt, you're off. You've done a grand job in the Regiment. Never thought about signing on, I suppose?'

'Yes Sir, but no thank you, Sir.'

'Got a good job to go to?'

'Yes Sir, Dockin'.'

'Dockin'?'

'Yes Sir, me father's a docker.'

'Good job is it?'

'Yes Sir; hundred quid a week.' This was 1956.

‘Good God. That sounds a very good job. Don’t you think so RSM? Perhaps you and I might apply?’

‘Don’t you worry Sir, no problem,’ said Lance-Corporal Mabbutt, ‘I’ll speak to me father.’

NINE

Civvy Street

My car packed with all that I possessed, including the two Old Etonian ties, blazer and scarf left to me by my father, I headed down that dreary road to the Hook of Holland and Harwich. At least I would never have to do this journey again. But where was I to go? I had little choice but to make for brother Lawrence in Sussex, there to form a base in his house near a little country town. He greeted me:

'So you've finished with your feather-bedded existence?'

'Feather-bedded?'

'You'll find out. Can't think why you didn't leave years ago and join me here. No worries, no tax, no bosses. Bliss. Have another drink. Joan dear, George is back.'

Her Ladyship let out a grunt. I had never liked her, nor she me. An expensive red-head adored by Lawrence, she rarely got out of bed in the mornings, and had done so hardly at all through the war, finding in my brother's absence that it was a most agreeable place to entertain during the allied occupation of the West End. He had married her, having assiduously pursued her sister for many months, the latter a woman of bodily perfection who, despite sharing her bed regularly, remained a frustrated virgin. Joan, having observed this charade with the watchfulness of the practised predator, invited him to try her instead. This he did and, finding her the more satisfactory, married her. Later their rows were to become as public as they were expensive: into a cold bath, never to recover, would go a mink coat; out of a taxi window would fly a gigantic emerald ring. Yet they remained largely content in their enmity, indifferent to the many other beds that became a way of life for them both.

'Yes, feather-bedded,' went on Lawrence. 'You joined the Army, hunted eight days a week, night-clubbed round London, had a little war, got promotion, commanded your Regiment; now you have a pension. I didn't want to join the Army. Quite spoilt my business and all I got was bloody shot and a demob suit that didn't fit.'

I had been very proud, cooped up in Warburg, to hear that Lawrence had shed Kennard blood. But I had never heard how it happened.

'Well actually, old boy, it was a brother Officer. We had a row in an Algerian night-club and the bugger shot me.' He paused reflectively. 'I imagine he might be nearly out of jail by now. Still, never mind all that. Why don't you join me in my business?'

Lawrence's business consisted almost wholly of punting heavily on horses and occasionally making a foray into ownership. He had a ticker-tape machine installed at his home and kept an eye on the racing results and, sometimes, on a stock-market which was a complete mystery to him. Thanks to Mama and our Grandmother Kennard, Lawrence had inherited a great deal of money which they had kept out of Coleridge's reach. He had also, it seemed, been left the Villa Mary Graham, a fact which somehow had escaped me up to now.

'What did you do with it?' I asked curiously.

'Flogged it. Funny little man turned up here with ten thousand smackers. All in notes. I needed the money for the business. Who wants a villa in the South of France anyway?' Somebody did want it though, for a few years later it was sold on for half a million pounds. It was only after Lawrence's death that I discovered that Papa had left a third of the Villa to me!

True to his word Lawrence had not invested the loot in any form recognized as security by the City of London:

'I just used it for the business. Come on, join me. You really can't go wrong.'

'Do,' said Joan, 'I need a new fur coat.'

'Don't worry,' said Lawrence, impatiently, 'I'll get you one tomorrow. It's Kempton.'

The next day I went with him to see the business at work. The camaraderie on the race-course is always delightful and even Lawrence's shiftier-looking friends were friendly as we bolted from bar to bar in search of 'information'.

'Don't talk to me while I'm in action,' he said, downing another huge whisky. 'I'll see you here before the three o'clock. I'll have something by then.'

He had. It came in at eight to one and I had won fifty quid.

'There you are,' he said. A wad of notes fell out of a hole in his pocket as we celebrated.

'Look out. You're losing all your money. It's there on the ground beside you.'

'Keep it,' he said airily, 'its no use to me. Come on, we've got to go and get Joan that new coat.'

'Don't like it much,' said his lady when we reached home. 'And hurry up, you're late; I've got ten people coming to dinner.'

One of them was Molly. She was delightful to look at, fun to talk to and a great pleasure to kiss; a splendid combination during and after the usual champagne and good food.

'Did you see Molly?' said Joan after they had all left. She was hazy with champagne. 'She sat next to George and never drank a thing.'

'Of course not,' I said. 'She doesn't drink. She told me.'

'Balls,' said Lawrence. 'She drinks like a fish. Come on, we must go to bed. Newbury tomorrow. I'm sorry you don't like the coat, darling. I'll get you something better.'

I didn't go to Newbury. I had made an assignation with

promises of more interesting times to come. We met and the promises were delightfully fulfilled. Neither of us needed a drink.

Molly was on the road to a divorce and there were two splendid children. They had all lived in Kenya where everyone had drunk rather a lot; that was in the past and no longer a problem. But, more important, what was I going to do? Surely I couldn't go on living with Lawrence and Joan, and surely I couldn't go into the business with him? No, I could not. I knew a little more than Lawrence about capital and income, but not much. And I had not much capital either.

What did I want to do? That was easy. I wanted to be able to afford to hunt and shoot and fish. And I needed badly the touch of a woman who wanted to feel me in her arms as I wanted to hold her in mine. I wanted, too, to enjoy the written words in my favourite books and to do so as the sun shone on scenes more lovely than could be caught by paint. I had long been aware that I miss what many gain from painting, and sculpture too. Old Masters seem to choose such hideous women – even the Mona Lisa looks so much like a governess inflicted on my youth – and landscapes have no windows to open to breathe the air. Mama, in her numerology period, had filled her London flat with the most modern of sculpted pieces to complement her lovely pictures and priceless first editions. All, except the books, had failed to fill me with the wonder that others felt. All went up with the bomb, and Lawrence got £5000 from the Government by way of compensation. It went into the business.

First I had to find a house and did so in Hook Norton, in the country where Ronnie Wallace, maestro of my favourite sport, hunted the Heythrop Hounds. I was able to buy forty acres too, and kept two horses brought back from Germany that loved their lives as I loved them. Together we took our fun in the heaven on earth that is hunting the fox.

'This is it, this it is, this is it . . .' The horse seems to pound out the beat as he gallops along in joy and in great endeavour. No game is worth a rap where there can be no misfortune, no mishap to mar a day. The fox running straight, the hounds speaking their excitement to their Master, a bigger bullfinch up ahead, steady, hup and over. Hooray. The unspeakable in pursuit of the uneatable.

Unspeakable? Those in this marvellous gallop? Those in elegant pink coats inherited from families who left fortunes to the RSPCA and care for animals unknown to those in urban terraces and universities? Banker, miner, soldier, farmer; all risking all in the pursuit of pleasure.

Uneatable? Indeed, and no enemy apart from man. The snare, the lingering death from shot-gun wounds, the choking, indiscriminate poisoned gas – or the chase where the advantage is with the hunted and where kills are few enough to give the lie to those who say it is not sport?

All this is part of England: John Peel and Jorrocks, the Fox and Hounds, the Duke of Beaufort; country inns that have heard the tales of the hunt that day. Rooted as much in the countryside as the terraces of Anfield and Old Trafford are rooted in the cities. Who would deny the frenzied happiness of those who follow in support of Liverpool? They too are the committed; no skulking indoors or on the fence for them. They and their country cousins will once more be there when the horn and whistle blow and England is again in need.

Meanwhile the urban fraternity spend happy days in the country paid to make a nuisance of themselves at meets by the antis. On this subject I wrote to *The Times* in May, 1983:

> *Political Manifestoes*
> Sir – To abolish Field Sports would cost several thousand jobs. To prohibit cheerful efforts to place hooks into fishes' mouths would cost several million votes. Is Mr Foot's dog too wet to chase a mouse?

To Hook Norton came Molly; we had been together much and she felt the need to make her position clear to the world: 'Darling, you treat me like a tart'. We went to a Registry Office in London, just she and I. We came out to find my car towed away to some strange pound and that our honeymoon plane could not wait. So small a thing can give such a bad start and we spent that night in no new pleasures, but drowned our celebrations – or was it sorrows – in too much drink.

Her income barely covered the education of her children and that was a constant source of worry to her. It must be the same for many, even though the queues for public schools seem to grow. I suspect that not many would regret the abandonment of private education. Certainly not the children who would instead inherit the money now used to buy their O and A Levels.

It had become urgent to earn some money. I thought that perhaps one of the horses might pay his way by racing. We would try. A great thrill: coming into the last in front and at 10 to 1. He broke his gentle leg there – and so did I. It seemed after all that I would have to earn his keep, not he mine.

The job market was very bleak. Redundant soldiers and ex-District Commissioners from distant territories newly independent were thick on the ground. I determined to make a military appreciation of the situation. I did so, and of the 'Courses Open' to me it seemed that a formal job was not a starter. I considered the newest crazes: mink, chinchilla, rabbits, chickens. 'Broilers is what you want,' proclaimed our local feed merchant, 'better than rabbits, they don't eat their young.' So broilers it was. Ten thousand of them in a 'controlled environment'. Happy when young, growing from day- to six-weeks-old, miserable in freezing lorries to the slaughter-house, they were hardly a great dish when frozen in cellophane. They covered the cost of producing that 'controlled environment', though scarcely paying for ours.

There were four of us now, with Molly's children, and two

ponies besides. It hardly required a business brain to see that the broilers would have to pull their fingers out if they were to pay bills other than their own. They couldn't: weight-for-feed remained a constant factor in their production and sufficient profit eluded me. I went to see Lawrence: 'Can't think why you don't join me, old boy. Things are going marvellously. I've bought two horses. Got them with Ron Smythe; helps the business a lot – I get tips from him.' In the small Sussex town, I noticed broilers revolving on machines called Rotis-o-mat; round and round, getting cooked. There were queues by each glass cooker. Hurrah, I had it; I had the Master Plan.

Back at home I bought a caravan. Hopeless with my hands, I invented a machine that went round and round and worked off calor gas. I took it, caravan and all, to a local Pony Club event. The queues formed; patient mothers, seeing that they no longer needed picnics, asked me to come again. No one complained of the price, three and six a quarter, including a packet of Smith's crisps. Couldn't I carry lemonade as well? I let them have free lemonade, the little darlings. Three and sixpence a quarter for a chicken costing seven bob didn't seem to need an accountant. I was home and dry, counting out greasy pound notes on the drawing-room carpet.

Those greasy notes rolled in as I travelled the county, doing the Shows and the Events. We bought another horse and employed a man. I sent him to Badminton, weighed down with quarters, crisps and lemonade. He telephoned: 'They won't let me in. They say we haven't got a concession. What's a concession? What shall I do, Sir?' I told him to withdraw and take the caravan to the car-park. Off he went, and soon sold out. Sweaty and triumphant, he arrived home with the greasy loot. By the next post came an indignant letter from a firm of caterers. What the hell did I think I was doing? I wrote humbly in reply: 'I am so sorry, I didn't know. My man told me and I told him to sit quietly in the car-park. He couldn't keep people away. Please forgive me. G. Kennard, Mobile Barbecues Ltd.'

By return came the reply: 'My dear Loopy, I didn't know it was you. You really must learn about concessions. You have a very good idea; perhaps you'd like to come and see me? We do the race-courses and might well use you. All the best, Len Livingstone-Learmonth, Managing Director, Letheby and Christopher.' A most delightful man, last seen trying to manoeuvre an antiquated artillery piece in Greece. Letherby and Christophers were then, as now, the leading race-course caterers.

Thus were race-course concessions laid before me, and the 3-Day Event at Badminton too. Badminton lasted only one year; so many quarters were eaten there by those walking the course in that wonderful park that the Duke of Beaufort's hounds abandoned foxes for cast-away chicken bones. Nevertheless a fortune lay ahead: we must buy more vans; employ more men. We went fishing while we thought.

There has to be a fortune at hand somewhere, if only in the distance, to fish the Spey. The most beautiful river in a land of beautiful rivers, the Spey moves majestically, sometimes turbulent over its rounded, rocky pools, sometimes placid as it drifts through pinewoods and banks of wild flowers. Oystercatchers voice their urgency and red squirrels watch from overhanging conifers. Within its peaty waters swim the salmon: swiftly, lazily, sulkily. Our beat was the Wester Elchies, most prized of all and presided over by Jimmy Milne, a wonderful man and a ghillie whose name is synonymous with Spey. Our fishing party was the same, year after year, as it is now; only incapacity or death, it seems, can break the spell. Then there was Scotty, the same who commanded me in Aldershot and led a fine armoured brigade under Montgomery at El Alamein. Usually fierce, always a sportsman, he had won the Kadir Cup, the blue riband of pig-sticking in India, three years running in the 1920s. Those cups still sit, with three more like them, in the Officers' Mess of the Regiment. He was supported always on the river by his wife, Patsy. On non-hunting days in the winter he made minnows, spinning lures, turning them out with squinting eyes. There was Cyanide Sid – 'I told you so' – of Warburg. Nothing but the best of equipment for Sid and he too made minnows. His had goo-goo eyes, and like Scotty's the fish treated them with disdain. With Sid was Judith his wife; and I had my Molly.

We were staying then, as we do now, at the little hotel in Archiestown, a delightful village with a proud war memorial carrying so many names from so small an area. After breakfast we went down to the river and made for the various pools. The dogs (more dogs than people) tore up and down chasing the countless rabbits – their success rate was often higher than ours. As the day was hot and bright, I decided to walk up the bank to see how Sid and Scotty were getting on. They would be fishing hard, I thought. Were they hell; they were sitting in a car whilst Sid showed off a new piece of kit, a fish tray for storing the fish he caught. Fat chance he had of putting it to any use while he sat in the car. Patsy and Judith were further up, trying to unstick a spinner from the bottom; spinning was allowed that day for the water was high and brown with the rains of the previous week.

A little later things had changed, but not much. This time it was Scotty showing off some new gadget: a gaff for catching the fish he caught, he explained to Sid. That someone else should have a piece of shiny equipment that he did not possess was too much for Sid and he went off to launch a fresh offensive during which he lost two Hardy spinners.

I went to look for Patsy. She had been hidden round a bend and none of us had seen that she was precariously balanced in the river with an angry fish buzzing about her, well and truly hooked. She had been shouting for help for half an hour and was turning grey with the effort. I dashed back to get the brand new gaff.

'Quick, Patsy's into a huge fish, give me the gaff.' The others, having as yet had no luck, were not prepared to be impressed.

'I'm not going to see her fish,' said Judith.

'Nor, I,' said Sid. 'It's just like the Casino this river. You decide how much kit you're going to lose and when you've had your lot you call it a day. Anyway she's probably caught the bottom again.'

Scotty got into the car with me. As we drove off we heard Judith saying wistfully that they might just stroll along and see what all the fuss was about.

Old habits die hard. I had a deep respect for Scotty and an affection, coupled with awe, for his wife. Whatever happened I was not going to lose that salmon. I jumped into the river clutching the gaff. After a struggle I landed the fish, huge, on the bank. Then I slipped and so did the fish – back into the water and away.

'God,' I said.

'Darling,' said Molly.

'Told you . . .' began Sid, who had just arrived. I looked at him and he stopped.

'Now she won't have to cook it,' murmured Judith. Patsy's face shone as if she'd had a revelation. She wore a look somewhere between that of a child deprived of a favourite teddy-bear and of a saint beaming forgiveness on the world. Scotty must have mellowed with the years because he kept his peace. Thank God, I thought as I retreated to the car. Thank God I am no longer subject to military law.

Quite soon after this most traumatic of incidents the water level dropped and we returned to the fly. Sid produced a pretty bottle, Japanese he assured us, and containing a completely irresistible salmon aphrodisiac. I tried it and it worked. There on the bank lay twenty pounds of shimmering elegance.

'Told you so,' said Sid.

A tap on the head and it died. In its staring eyes I seemed

to see the years of travel and mystery, beyond the ken of man. Sid and Scotty are both dead now, their exploits known and revered by many. Their straightforward lives took no secrets to the grave in the way that salmon did.

Roll on, beloved Spey. Your grandeur will outlive man and your fish will be there for generations to come. Men, and women too, will long continue to cast a fly on Delagyle and Pol Na Cree, on Schuan and the Rhynd. A grey wagtail will ever sit on the rock called Big Pig and chatter out defiance to the wading fishermen, as its ancestors have done beyond our memory. Roll on beloved Spey.

Not long ago a friend to whom we had given a Spey salmon resurrected it from the deep-freeze for a very special dinner party. It was cooked and decorated before being allowed to cool on the kitchen table. There, a happy household cat found and sampled it before being disturbed. Luckily little damage was done; the fish was turned over and redecorated and a grand time was had by all. After dinner the hostess was horrified to find the cat dead by the Aga cooker. She rang her doctor, a family friend who, not a little worried by the suddeness of the cat's death, arranged that the whole dinner party should meet him at the cottage hospital where he would supervise a general stomach-pump. That disagreeable proceeding over, the party returned home for much-needed glasses of brandy. A little later the hostess's daughter arrived back from another party:

'Mummy darling, I'm so sorry; poor Moggy got run over. I put her by the Aga to get better but I see the poor old thing's dead.'

Home again at Hook Norton, we set about expanding our outlets and taking on more staff. The outlets were not a problem. Len Livingstone-Learmonth confirmed the racecourse franchise and we also started doing door-to-door trade in the manner of ice-cream vans; in the evenings Women's Institute meetings, far and wide, kept us busy. For staff I drew on my legacy of Army friends: some were rich, some very rich, but most were poor, and a lot had been made redundant compulsorily when the Army shrunk dramatically in 1958.'Great, Loopy; I'd love to do the race-courses.'

This from 'Screwy' Wright who had been a prisoner with me. He had escaped by first pretending that he was mad (a disguise easily assumed by Screwy) and then breaking out of his loony-bin in a POW striped night-shirt. He wandered about the German countryside for days in this lunatic garb until someone noticed and he was recaptured. He was the camp bookmaker, loved racing, and won riding at Cheltenham after the war, at the age of 53. Now he was to swop a tank and a horse for a chicken van: 'Great, Loopy.'

The chicken band-wagon rolled. When Fred Winter won, he would give all the jockeys in his race a free meal – and he often won. We branched out into London, feeding debs in their flats and called this enterprise 'Look, Why Cook'; even *The Times* ran an article headlined 'Cavalry Colonel Cooks the Chicken'. It was too good to last, and it didn't.

Somehow we never quite got to grips with the financial nuances. There was the question of how the staff, mostly friends, were to be paid during the vastly reduced work-load of the winter months. In practice people were not so much paid as encouraged to take what was due to them at the end of a successful day.

'Had a wonderful day at Ascot, Loopy, sold out. Only thing is, I'm afraid I backed one or two losers. Still, don't worry, I'll pay you back soon.' Incidents like that didn't seem to matter much, (except to the tax man who completely failed to appreciate such unorthodox business practices) as I counted out endless greasy pound notes. But I had to find a winter market.

I tried Woolworth. They liked the thought of doing away with their own smelly machines and having the cooked article delivered. They gave me three shops to practice on. It was another success. Before the vans returned they were on the telephone for more. This bubble grew as the others had, and then it, too, burst. Our chickens begun to be returned unsold. Worse, some had been sold as they were going off; suddenly no one wanted to know. Mobile Barbecues was on the slide.

On the slide, too, was brother Lawrence. In fact he'd reached the bottom of his particular slope before the chickens turned nasty. At the latest of his lavish house parties for Goodwood, it had been brought home to him that the well had at last run dry. His one remaining horse, aptly called Last Attempt, ran and came second, beaten a short head. 'Darling,' he said to Joan, 'I had my last penny on that horse.' It was true; and not just his money but the house and its contents too.

It didn't seem to worry Lawrence much; he'd seen the chicken vans about and reckoned he could manage one easily. It certainly didn't worry Joan who announced that she was decamping to London to find a 'richer, rather more reliable man'. It worried Molly though, for Lawrence would have to come and stay with us. I didn't think her concern altogether fair; after all we had stayed with them when we had nowhere to go. But Molly had been a little odd of late. I had first put it down to the natural distaste that any beautiful woman might have to being surrounded always by the smell of roasting chicken and the sight of wall-to-wall greasy pound notes. She somehow seemed worse when her children came home.

'What's wrong with Mummy?' I didn't know.

Lawrence soon got the hang of the Woolworth run and extended our activities to Fine Fare – and a number of pubs en route. The pubs were his undoing, for many times he had to be retrieved from a ploughed field, clutching his quota of pound notes. Eventually he lost his driving licence and at about the same time Joan returned complaining that 'They all seemed to be married'; her manhunting skills had deserted her. I didn't feel that I could have them both at Hook Norton

9. Myself on Rosso, who I rode
for the British Army Show-Jumping Team.

10. The Mobile Barbecue's Transport Company.

11. Nic.

12. Old Comrade's Dinner, 1959.
Prince Philip, myself, Major Pierson, Sir Winston Churchill.

so I moved them to a flat in the local Rectory. I had never seen Lawrence so happy. He worked hard and loved his customers. They too loved him and, while it lasted, his part of the business thrived, give or take the cash that would never quite tally.

I thought that the move would make Molly happier and less odd. Instead she became odder; gentle and kind in the mornings, a little peculiar by lunch-time and almost bizarre in the evenings. She had become a secret drinker and worse – an alcoholic.

We were to have a children's tea-party. Molly had gone to bed after lunch and I let her sleep on until it neared the time for the guests to arrive. I went to wake her and saw the pills. Rushing to hospital we were only just in time; the doctor confirmed that the dose was lethal. 'Odd' was no longer the word; just terribly sad. How could I not have guessed? Even if I had not been so busy trying to keep the business steady and desperately trying to regularize the accounts, would I have seen it? I believe not; it is after all so easy to hide a bottle in the cistern and take its contents neat, and she was wonderfully clever at appearing always to be sober and beautiful. Not drunk, it had seemed, but a little odd.

There were more pills and more ambulances and more 'only just in time'. Most poignantly, she always came back determined that she would conquer this hideous illness, and always within a week her will would collapse. There is no cure, but there is a God and there is Alcoholics Anonymous. Between them they raised my lovely Molly from the gutter.

At about the time that the writing on the wall began to spell out the final obituary for Mobile Barbecues, Lawrence arrived one morning to load his van.

'George,' he said, 'would you go round and have a look at Joan? I think she's dead.'

'She's what . . .?'

'Dead. I think she's dead. I can't wake her up.'

He went off on his round looking faintly depressed. I drove over to the Rectory and there in bed was Joan, stiff and rapidly going stiffer. I did the usual things and awaited the return of my brother. He'd had a good day and was slightly drunk. I sent him to bed (not the same bed) and went to answer the door-bell. It was the local Detective Inspector.

'May I see Sir Lawrence, Sir?'

'He's just gone to bed, Inspector, upset and a little drunk. Must you see him now?'

'Yes, if you please.' He looked at me. 'You can stay if you like.'

I went to wake him. Lawrence was not pleased:

'Good God, what the hell does he want? Bad enough losing one's wife without seeing a detective.'

Eventually I persuaded him to come downstairs and he arrived, hiccupping gently. The Inspector was polite and deferential. He was also insistent that Lawrence should answer his questions. After a few preliminaries, he came to the nub of the matter.

'Can you tell me, Sir, what you and Lady Kennard did last night?'

'Nothing really. We had a very happy evening. Watched television, rather a good play. And then we went to bed.'

The Inspector wrote it all down, turned back a few pages of his note-book and looked up. Lawrence hiccupped.

'I see,' said the policeman, 'that the Vicar says that he heard you and Her Ladyship screaming at each other at about 11.30p.m. He says he heard Lady Kennard shouting that she hated your bloody guts and wished she'd never married you. He also says that she repeated that she loathed you, several times.'

'Oh,' said Lawrence, 'you don't want to take any notice of that. We always talked to each other like that. Doesn't mean a thing. Can I go to bed now?' He turned to me: 'I'll do the Bristol run tomorrow, George.'

After he had swayed off upstairs, I told the Inspector that it was true that they did always talk to each other like that and that I was quite sure that there was no question of Lawrence murdering his wife. The Inspector closed his book noncommittally and said that of course he understood but that there would have to be further enquiries. On this disconcerting note he left.

As the weeks went by, Lawrence worked hard and seemed happy. The Inspector had returned to ask him to account for some blood that had been found on the bed sheets and Lawrence had told him that his bitch had been on heat and often bled on the bed. So it proved.

It was several weeks before the inquest was held. This my brother attended with a whisky flask in his pocket. No doubt the Court assumed that it was grief that caused him to bury his head in his hands quite so often. Sitting next to him I knew better. The verdict was 'Open', and remains so to this day.

Lawrence's hiccupping, which had started when the Inspector called, began to recur frequently. So severe did they become that he was taken to hospital for an exploratory operation; it was suspected that he had an ulcer. But he had no ulcer; he was riddled with cancer and they sewed him up and sent him home to die. It was easy to pretend that his ulcer meant that he should stop drinking. It was equally easy to connive with his attempts to keep a bottle of whisky under the sheets so that he could have a swig when his Nurse, ('the old bag') wasn't looking. Particularly easy as she was in on the secret. In the end he died, not of cancer, but as a result of a progressively merciful course of morphine. To the last he followed his beloved horses. On the morning of his death he asked me to put a fiver on Little Willy at Ascot. Knowing that this day was probably his last, I thought it right to venture a hundred. At tea-time, he regained consciousness:

'Did it win, old boy?' Unthinkingly, I said it hadn't.

'Fuck,' he said, and then he died. If humanity is a passport to heaven, he is surely there.

He had hundreds of acquaintances but no real friends. None came to his funeral; just his bookie and me. I loved him.

I was now faced with winding up Mobile Barbecues. There seemed to be an awful lot of creditors and, unbusinesslike to the end, I determined that they should all be paid. Hook Norton had to go. I managed to keep the cottage and stabled my horse in its garage. But he had to be fed and I needed a job.

I reviewed my assets: an upbringing that despised commerce, (but I had come to terms with that); an expert on flogging chickens; references from Churchill and Wavell; 50 years old. It didn't seem too bad but there were still a great many ex-soldiers and former colonial administrators on the market.

My first interview was not a success. It was conducted by a horrible little man in spectacles, the manager of a local branch of a national company.

'So you were a Lieutenant-Colonel were you? Well let me tell you we don't much like Lieutenant-Colonels here. There are no Other Ranks in civilian life, you know.'

I told him that I had come across no finer body of men than Other Ranks, and if there were none in his company, then he was the loser. Nonetheless I toured the factory briefly with him and was amused to see a loo marked 'Manager Only'! The work-force (no Other Ranks) was bent to its various tasks. There wasn't a single 'Good-Morning'; no smiles; no 'How's the wife, Bill?'. I left depressed and sometimes wonder whether that manager and the many like him that I was to meet subsequently, are now among the senior hierarchy of the CBI; I do hope not.

At Portland House, home of cement, things were delightfully different. A cheerful Hall Porter showed me the way to the seventeenth floor. Victor Elison, the Managing Director, rose from behind his vast desk set in front of even vaster windows, and greeted me – and the Hall Porter. I burbled about my references but he said not to worry about them, what had I done? Ah yes, he had seen the chicken vans, jolly good they were too. What did I know about cement? That was easy – nothing. Would I mind putting on an overall and learning? Longing to. He called in his Sales Manager, Norman Mullins, another delightful man. Let's all have a drink. What did I like to be called? Loopy, eh; well why not?

The interview concluded, we went downstairs. Waving away his Rolls, he got into his Mini and roared off to lunch. The Porter hovered. How had it gone? He hoped I'd got the job. Lovely company this and a lovely boss. Did I know he'd got a DSO and an MC in the war? I didn't but I might have guessed. Two days later I got a letter telling me to report to the factory on the first of the next month. Hurrah.

So began the idlest time of my life. The factory at Beddington was not a cement plant but manufactured the company's special products: Snowcem, Sandtex and other household brands. I was to be initiated into their fabrication, their application and their hundred and one vagaries and my instructor was a foreman called George Barnes who *always* said 'Good Morning' and everybody said 'Good Morning' to him. He had been a Company Sergeant Major during the war and had clearly been as loved and respected then as he was now at Beddington. He set himself – and others – the highest of standards and he led by example. He would give me some decorating project with a new product with which I had to become familiar; when the tea bell rang he would be hovering to see that I downed tools with the rest.

'We don't want everybody out on strike just 'cos you don't want your tea, now do we?'

Thus he nannied his supremely inept pupil. He was angry with me only once and that was when I called him George in front of his apprentices. I was never to do that again. 'Mr Barnes' it was to be in public – always.

In this way I became a fully-fledged representative for Blue Circle Cement, complete with company car. It was going to be easier to feed my horse now that I no longer had to feed my own car as well. We Blue Circle reps ranged all over England, crawling down country lanes and speeding on the motorways as our suits got shinier and our vehicles rattled with company wares. We were a happy bunch and proud of our products.

My patch was the Midlands and my targets were builders' merchants, architects (in our company language, RIBA stood for Remember I'm a Bloody Architect) and Local Authorities. I spent my days travelling and meeting people and yet it was often lonely. To make a 'Call', I arrived and waited; waited some more and eventually made contact. Sometimes I even made a sale, but mainly I just waited. It occurred to me, in some Town Clerk's outer office, that, as I was now a Baronet, that fact might be turned to a tangible advantage in the way that 'Lieutenant-Colonel' clearly could not be. I had called several times at a particularly depressing set of municipal offices and, as plain Kennard, had not even managed an audience, although I had been given ample opportunities to catch up on the latest editions of *Titbits*. I approached the harridan at the desk (she was new and hadn't seen me before):

'Please tell Mr Smith that Sir George Kennard would like to see him at his earliest convenience.'

I was swept in without a moment's delay.

'Good morning, Sir George. Have we, in fact, met before? Would you like a cup of coffee? What can I do for you?' I gulped down my coffee and broke the bad news that I had come to flog him some Sandtex. He remained courteous and there are still numerous walls in an otherwise unlovely Midlands town that are covered in that most excellent of materials.

At a race meeting at Ascot, sponsored by Blue Circle, I was

detailed to look after two Afghan princes. Rashly, I asked them down to Devon to shoot. They arrived, having just purchased two Purdey shotguns. Since there is nothing much here to shoot I frantically asked a Colonel who ran a syndicate shoot nearby if I could bring them. They were greeted by the Colonel who told them that their ancestors had shot his grandfather in the Afghan war. They nearly shot the Colonel, but enjoyed their day. A massive cement order followed, was paid for, and rotted uncollected in the Gulf.

I stayed with the Company for ten years and learnt a lot. I learnt to respect top management in British industry and was confirmed in my view that the working man is as fundamentally decent and hard-working as any of his forebears, especially when he works for a company that cares about him as an individual. I learnt with a sadness which sometimes amounted to despair how easy it was for the most honest and straightforward of men to be driven into the arms of politically motivated trade-union officials by the incompetence and uncaring nature of junior and middle management, whose only motivation often appeared to be to distance themselves from those they were supposed to be leading.

During the period when some company directors (not my company) were awarding themselves huge pay rises, I wrote the following letter to *The Times*, which resulted in my receiving an invitation to join the Communist Party:

> *Other People's Wages*
> Sir – Proud to be English, born a Conservative, I am happy to be wage-frozen if it helps the country for which many of my contemporaries died. I work in a modest position for a national company for which I have total respect. Should, however, my Chairman be awarded a £16000 a year rise and I £2 a week, I would consider that my country was going mad and that my

> company deserved no respect. I would be
> delighted to go on strike and my vote would be
> socialist and left of left.

While I was finding my feet in cement, Molly was being rescued, as finally as these things can ever be, by Alcoholics Anonymous. But we had drifted apart; the strain of winding up the chickens, selling Hook Norton, paying the debts, finding a job and doing it, and trying to understand her had spelt the end of another marriage. I gave her the cottage and bolted to Devon with the Incredibly Wonderful Woman who is now my wife.

TEN

Devon

Nicola lived in London, but her family home is at Warnicombe in Devon on a hill near Tiverton. There lived Ruth, her mother, a daughter of the Chamberlain family of Birmingham and Munich fame, who had married a Devonian squire, Peter Carew. He, badly wounded at Gallipoli, and knowing nothing of business, had been sucked into the Birmingham enterprises to play a major part in running Tube Investments.

Peter and Ruth had two children, but Tim, their son, and Nicola were involved in an appalling motor accident from which Tim later died, so putting an end to what had already been a brilliant career at Oxford.

Nic had been married to Charles Breitmeyer, a lawyer by whom she had four boys, before divorce claimed that union too. Divorce these days is common in a way which it then was not and I am sufficiently modern (or immoral?) to commend it when co-habitation becomes constant conflict; but it is unjust indeed when a woman alone is saddled with the futures of four sons.

Gogwell farmhouse, on the Warnicombe estate, had been prepared by Ruth for Nic and the boys to escape to at weekends, but we now decided to make it our home. The understanding company for whom I worked agreed to transfer me from the Midlands to their South-West region, where I continued to badger Town Clerks into Snowceming everything in sight, and took on the management of Gogwell farm.

The divorce proceedings and subsequent events had hit the

boys hard and I saw it as my role to try and stabilize their lives and bring a little fun. Hugo, then aged 18, Peter, Henry and Geoffrey all hit it off with Zandra and her children from the beginning and are now all married to delightful wives; Nic's grandchildren are increasing at an alarming rate.

Hugo, having achieved the distinction of a first at Exeter University and a Doctorate at London, lives close by. Peter thrilled me by joining my Regiment and then going on to Oxford where he became president of the Bullingdon Club and engaged in dangerous sports, hurling himself off the Golden Gate Bridge in San Fransisco attached to an elastic band. It was the beginning of yuppiedom then and he succumbed to the lure of City money, never again settling to the military life.

Peter and his friends courted some publicity during their pursuit of lunatic activities, but nothing approaching that in which Henry found himself involved. Henry had done well, working his way up from washing dishes to a responsible position with a national food and drink company, when a friend in London conceived the notion that it would be possible to interest the BBC in subsidizing a fishing trip to Scotland to catch a monster skate. The resulting film would be called *The Fishing Party*. Henry fell hook, line and sinker (unlike, as it turned out, the skate) and four young men set off in the company of a film crew and a producer whose avowed intent it was to capture the party's views on life, politics and sport. This was a recipe for disaster and so it turned out. Inept comments, some made seriously, most flippantly, were extracted by questions (not heard on the programme) posed by the producer who frequently complained that answers were not controversial enough. Displays of bad manners were staged and manipulated and the film was inter-cut with scenes of deprivation and social riot. In the absence of the skate, the film director enticed seagulls close to the fishing boat from which the party was shooting at tin cans in the sea. Inevitably a gull was shot (by the only non-countryman of the four) and much was made of it. On return from Scotland they all came to Gogwell to film further background material and Nic gave them lunch. They, in turn, gave us a hidden microphone left live at the dining-room table whilst the BBC team went into the garden to shoot exteriors. In my resultant row with the mandarins of Broadcasting House, they claimed that the microphone had been left on accidentally!

This was not the first row I had had with the BBC. In May, 1981, some pictures from Ulster were shown on BBC television which shocked the nation. I wrote as follows to *The Times*:

> *Martyrs of Ulster*
> Sir – Will the television crew who stood by, filming one of Her Majesty's soldiers running towards them with his uniform on fire (BBC 1 News, 13 May) and shouting in agony for help, now get some 'suitable' reward?

There was a great deal of reaction, in *The Times* and elsewhere. The television reporter, Kate Adie, found it necessary to defend herself in an article in the same newspaper occupying six column-inches. The cameraman wrote to me putting his point of view. In essence this (and Adie's) was that it was better that trained soldiers and policemen should be left to deal with the situation unhampered by well-meaning civilians, and that horrific pictures of this nature helped to produce awareness of the troubles.

To go back to my new family, of Geoffrey I entertained high hopes that he would eventually follow Peter into the Regiment but it was not to be; at Bristol University he met the gorgeous Max and soon they were married. At Bristol he formed The Alternative Dangerous Sports Club and took on the Clifton suspension bridge with an elastic band every bit as insecure as Peter's in America. For their honeymoon Max and Geoffrey went to Chile where they rode ponies up uncharted routes in the Andes and adopted a dog of mixed ancestry and unbounded devilment. Geoffrey devotes his energies to developing property, mainly in France, from an apparently not inconvenient base in Oxford.

It was not always so, and I include my letter to him in his undergraduate days (in sympathy to undergraduate parents).

My dear Geoffrey,

You will have received your mother's letter, and you will note that your party for next weekend is restricted to four. It is not a penalty imposed on you; it is that your elder brothers have asked the maximum that this small house and little shoot can take.

I have given you before a perhaps much-resented lecture on 'reining back'. At the time it seemed to register, and was received with your usual charm, and then totally neglected in what I consider a Disastrous weekend. Should you, with your usual conceit, be amazed at the word Disaster I will attempt to outline my complaints.

It should be a delight to have you and your friends at home, with all the pleasure that gun and horse can offer whenever you choose. But you are to remember, and see that your friends remember, that this is a civilised house and demands civilised behaviour and that your friends enjoy what there is to offer with a modicum of upbringing and good manners. Presumably, if no example is set by you and you will happily chew your meat with your fingers, your guests will continue to spit orange pips on to the floor and discard their burning cigarettes onto the dining room carpet. Such antics may be welcome in your flat, and there they may prove their manhood by drinking to their fatuous hearts' content, but here – no more. They will receive the normal courtesy, at our expense, of pre-meal drinks and wine for supper, and they are welcome to the comforts of the drawing room if they can refrain from littering the furniture with wet glasses and can exert themselves sufficiently to stand up and offer your mother a chair when she comes into the room. You will also see that she has time to do so, by either clearing the table yourself, or press-ganging your open-mouthed half-wits to help as well. Maybe they come from Butler-Footmen households; you don't. And since I flatly refuse to wet-nurse a collection of incompetent undergraduates the onus falls on your Mama. Not only will you help her, even if it detracts from your non-existent dignity, but you will let her know, well in advance, how many are coming, and when, that food may be got out of the deep freeze and eaten at the normal time by those who are present and not by those who have the discourtesy to arrive late and expect to be fed and wined. You will also stop helping yourself to food whenever you feel like it, cigarettes wherever you find them, and bottles of spirits at your convenience. Certainly if the lot of you cannot communicate without the aid of alcohol you may retire to the barn, but you will buy your own cigarettes and your own drink. You will manage to smoke the former with the aid of an ashtray, and you will inebriate yourselves happily without breaking glasses and driving over a lawn to frighten a grandmother from whom the source of 'Your Money' has entirely come. You will sleep in the bedrooms that are allotted and you and your guests will exert themselves to turn out the lights. Those young men who come to shoot will bring their own guns and cartridges, or offer to buy them here, and come suitably clad without raiding our cupboards. And should you wish to borrow my car you will return it in the same state with gratitude and not a litter of loose cartridges and cigarette ends that no doubt 'somebody else will clear up'. It would also seem necessary to inform them that it is customary to leave some small tip to the unfortunate 'Daily'.

You are now comfortably off. There can be few undergraduates with a flat and a Diane Citröen. Any further money will depend on your ultimate earning capacity, and should you continue to treat your car as you appear to be so doing there will be no question of 'Mummy, can I have another car?'

Think on these things, Geoffrey dear, or ignore them at your peril. You may believe the 'Idiot Boy' act may be attractive. There are many, like me, the chauvinistic pig, who think differently.

In 1980 I retired from the great cement company and devoted my time to the 450 acres. Under my careful management the overdraft increased alarmingly and the annual interest, the wages bill and the need to maintain expensive machinery made it imperative that a solution be sought. There appeared to be three alternatives: selling (never – the Carews have been in Devon since Domesday); giving up the freehold and leasing the land; or exploring the newest invention in the agricultural world, share farming. A scheme was put to us by a local, and most efficient, land agent who then drew up the necessary agreement to be signed by us and two keen young men who arrived with their charming families. The overdraft was cut by two-thirds overnight and the wage-bill went to provide for the partners. Those 450 acres now seem to support three families, not in luxury perhaps, but in harmony and happiness.

I find harmony and happiness still in the English countryside not yet abused by developers. Its beauty remains, as does its sport with horse and gun and rod. We ran a horse this year in our local point-to-point, ridden to my great delight by my grandson. It was touch and go whether we could use our dilapidated lorry – a blackbird had nested in the engine and hatched Eenie, Meenie, Minie and Mo. The fledglings were loath to leave the nest but did so just in time, except poor Mo who fell down the carburettor. On arrival at the course I presented myself to the Secretary's tent to declare the horse, to be told by an otherwise engaging woman that I needed to produce a passport for the animal. I explained that this was not a foreign horse, not even an Arab's, but English born and bred. I saw no need for a passport. I said that in my day not only members but members' horses were readily recognized. They let us run (we reached only the third fence) but had to do their duty and report me to the Authorities. I wrote in mitigation and received a letter of forgiveness asking me please to read the rules. Ah, read the rules. I should have done that more carefully all my life.

Read the rules? Eilen Roc and the Villa Mary Graham were occupied in sorry sequence by French, German and American armies. Within their walls there must have been many treasures from an epoch when painters, whose works now fetch many millions of pounds chose to live in an area dominated by my grandmother, a great patron of the arts. All had 'vanished' – save one, in England – a painting called Ahab and Jezebel by Lord Leighton. An art dealer told me,

'Loopy, you must get it back. It hangs in Scarborough Museum and is worth £200,000.'

This was a fortune that I badly need, so I bolted to the solicitors who made my grandmother's will. Next to Claridge's, where she had lived her last few years, Boodle Hatfield welcomed me to their smart interview room, surrounded with imposing paintings and a book on the History of Boodle Hatfield.

Yes, I was the sole inheritor of Mrs Carew's art and trust jewellery.

'Trust jewellery? It's all missing'.

Hadn't I read the small print in the will, dissolving them from responsibility in such matters?

'But I know where some of it is. In Daphne Fielding's book *The Duchess of Jermyn Street* she writes, "Rosa loved jewellery. She had some magnificent pieces given to her by Sir Coleridge Kennard." And I have a letter from the late Duke of Kent thanking my father for the magnificent brooch he gave Marina on her wedding.'

Oh well, nothing can be done about that. But what about the Leighton picture which now hangs at Scarborough?

'Sir George, we are a very expensive firm, but we will try and find out.'

They didn't, but Scarborough did. I had their receipt for £150 from Boodle's in my pocket.

Tension in that smart elegant room was getting stronger.

'You must realize, Sir George, we were only Mrs Carew's solicitors. It was the Trustees' responsibility'.

Trustees? Who was the chief trustee? Mr Boodle.

An old soldier friend of mine once took his solicitor into Hyde Park and debagged him. Colonel Wintle had some sympathy in the media for his action. Mine was milder. I took Counsel's Opinion.

'Not much hope old boy. Too long ago.'

Bill – £500.

Not long ago I took Nic, Zandra and my granddaughter Louise to Eilen Roc and walked that lovely stretch of coast that might have been mine, and marvelled at the beauty of the facade of the house that Coleridge loved and lost. We walked, too, down the Avenue James Wyllie in old Antibes and I dreamt again of the age of elegance. Soon after our return Zandra wrote the words addressed to her grandfather across the years that appear as an epilogue to this, my story.

The blackbirds around this small Devon house are no longer drunk. The cows no more take fright at a mini-plane, though the dogs become disturbed at the clattering of computers. Only the constant whirring of the washing machine still fed by my wife after the weekend remains the same.

'Let me look back upon the world before I leave it, and upon some scattered graves . . . Memory, thou hast not always been so kind as thou art now.'

I am told that when one 'snuffs it' the first one sees is one's favourite dog, wagging its tail. Hmmm! I think I had better go and mow the lawn.

EPILOGUE

Immortality Unthinkable?

My dear Grandpapa – or maybe I should say Grandpere? You see, I don't even know how to begin. How do you write to someone you never met, across the barrier of time gone by?

They said you had no interest in children – yet how could you write so hauntingly of childhood? Would they not have had a point of contact, that child at the beginning of Life; that man near the end?

I was six and you were still alive. They said you had no wish to see me. Later, I heard tell of a place called Monte Carlo, full of addictive gambling tables. Of that House, gone in a night; Of beauty spurned, and love lost on a rock; of drugs and degeneration. The sketch thus drawn was not a pretty one.

Yet now I find, among old papers, that you wrote of fairy stories, and so gently of a childhood Home you lost. They never told me of despair: I might have understood – you see, I too have loved a House . . .

You know, I'm sure – we have been back. Now I have seen your Eilen Roc.

Old ghosts came out and walked the avenues that day. They laughed up at us from the rocks, and I think there was a boy who paused to watch us, as we wandered by. It was hard to see, shading one's eyes against the dazzling azure sea.

It is good to know that the House is well kept and the grounds carefully tended. For what? For civic duties, for a display of grandeur from those former days. And yet, the House seemed almost to be waiting. Was it aloof to our curious intrusion, or did it perhaps feel a sense of kinship?

And you – did you give a damn that we should want to trace old roots? Perhaps you shrugged and turned away, not wishing to see any more.

Or did you watch us at St Tropez, as we lunched outside in the sun?

He wore his Old Etonian tie, somewhat tattered at the ends, to stroll along the boulevard. Unusually tidy, it was a kind of salutation, an acknowledgement perhaps? The shades of an elegant and past brilliant age reached out then and touched the afternoon.

They did not understand, those passers-by, in gaudy shirts and skin-tight jeans. The glittering gin palaces, straining at their moorings, seemed paradoxically cheap and tawdry. Only the classic lines of the boat, with her wooden deck and fittings, seemed somehow in keeping, against the dark blue sea.

We sat and watched the world go by at Cannes – a somewhat different scene from that you used to view, no doubt. No gently swaying landaus now; the traffic-cluttered Promenade des Anglais can best be seen today by overflying . . .

Along the Boulevard James Wyllie: that little villa on the rocks – does it keep its sadness from the present owner? It is heavily barricaded now – against intrusion from the present – or the past?

We went, that last day, to Monte Carlo. Were you there, in the plush Casino, to watch your great-granddaughter Louise try her luck? Was it your cunning hand that let her win those first three throws? Did you see the sparkle in her eyes, and turn the wheel of fortune against her then, quelling a fatal flaw before it ever caught a hold?

I left the following day – leaving behind the azure sea, and something of myself, and flew home over the snowy Esterels.

Does it matter to you to know that, although the House is now in other hands, you left a legacy of sorts?

Have you really thrown your pen to me across the intervening years?

So tentatively I pick it up; so clumsily begin to form the words . . .

I wonder –

Your Granddaughter.

APPENDIX

The Beastliness of War

The history of the Second World War has been heavily overlaid by examples of German cruelties perpetrated on the Jews, on the occupied peoples and on prisoners of war. Most are well documented, few, if any, are exaggerated, and none have lacked extensive and often enthusiastic media coverage. The inclination towards self-flagellation enjoyed by the German persona has ensured that, even in Germany, publicity for such events has been unflagging in the cause of national atonement. I have often thought it monstrously unfair that the whole of the German people, and in particular the soldiers, sailors and airmen of the Third Reich, should be tarred by the same brush as the war criminals. I have also been astonished by the unspoken but general assumption that the Allies' behaviour was on all occasions faultless, albeit mitigated by sporadic acknowledgements that that of the Russians was not always what it might have been.

Towards the end of the nineteen-seventies three former SS Colonels attempted to come to England to promote the publication of a book. There was the predictable outcry from the tabloid press and others keen to pick over the bones of the Nazi carcass. I wrote the following letter to *The Times* pointing out that the behaviour of the officers and soldiers of the Waffen SS Division against whom we fought in Greece was in the highest traditions of warfare and that only when we prisoners fell into the hands of non-combatant prison guards did standards fall considerably:

> *Refurbishing the SS Image*
> Sir – I had the honour to command Churchill's old regiment, the 4th Queen's Own Hussars. We were opposed to the Waffen SS for the whole of the Greek campaign. We found them magnificent soldiers and very fair fighters.
>
> History, after so many years, should be the truth.

Among the resultant mail (overwhelmingly supporting my view) was a letter from Richard Schulze-Kossens who had been Hitler's ADC during most of the last three years of the war. He had fought in Greece and thanked me for the sentiments expressed in the letter. Although not a journalist, a neo-fascist or an historian I thought this too good an opportunity to miss and responded to his invitation to visit him at his home in Düsseldorf.

Schulze-Kossens had been Ribbentrop's aide at the signing of the Hitler-Stalin pact and had found him a 'boring, humourless man'. He had then been a Colonel in the Adolf Hitler SS Division opposed to us in Greece. He was anxious to stress the essential difference between the political SS and the Waffen, or military, SS whose name, at least in the early stages of the war was synonymous with the exceptional military efficiency and solid camaraderie of all crack troops. Finally he was appointed to Hitler's personal staff.

Remembering my own days with Wavell, whom I loved, I asked:

'Did you love the man?'

'Of course.'

'Right until the end?'

'No. After the 29th July plot he was never the same. He had gone mad. He was also very deaf then and difficult to talk to.'

'As you were so very close to him, could you speak your own thoughts freely?'

'Most of the time. He was sometimes very angry if he had not been told the truth. Then it was difficult, perhaps dangerous, to speak to him.'

'Why did he not surrender when the war was clearly lost? It would have saved many lives and prevented much suffering.'

'He told me that he could not accept unconditional surrender; he could hope only for a political solution.'

'Did he discuss this with the General Staff?'

'Many times. Rommel told him that there was no other solution other than surrender. Hitler replied that it was his job to fight and to leave the political decisions to his Führer.'

'Were you not horrified at Rommel's death?'

'Yes. He was not actively involved with the plot. Speidel implicated him.'

'Apart from Rommel, could the other senior officers speak their minds? What about Keitel for instance, and Jodl?'

'Always. Provided that it was the truth. Hitler hated a situation to be painted in rosier colours than it actually was.'

'How did you regard von Stauffenberg?'

'Most people now think of him as a hero. I do not think so. He had many chances to kill Hitler when they walked together in the woods. He could have shot him then. Instead he planted a bomb, taking care that he would escape even though he knew that some of his friends and sympathizers could be killed by that bomb.'

'All the books and papers I have read mention that Hitler would rant and rave at conferences and even eat the carpet in rage.'

'I, too, have read these books and although I was always at Hitler's side for nearly three years, I never saw him rant, except when he was not told the truth. There are many inaccuracies in those books, even in Speer's. I wrote and told him so.'

'What about Bormann? Did he escape?'

'He was a most unpleasant man. I am nearly certain that he took poison.'

'How could you tolerate the existence of the concentration camps and the appalling cruelties inflicted on the Jews?'

'I knew nothing of this. I had access to all Hitler's papers and I never saw or heard any reference to concentration camps. I knew, of course, that it was Hitler's intention to solve the Jewish problem by settling them in Russian territory. All the occupied countries were expelling their Jews and sending them to the East. I did not know of the camps, only that Himmler had told Hitler that he would deal with the problem. Hitler never spoke of it and it was only after the war that we learnt what had happened.'

It is difficult to believe that a man at the very centre of affairs should have been quite so ignorant of events so momentous, but in the tortuous world of Adolf Hitler's Thousand Year Reich perhaps even that was possible. I questioned him later about the murder of escaping RAF prisoners towards the end of the war and he had no answer. He asked me why it had been necessary to carpet-bomb Dresden in the dying days before surrender, and I had no answer.

I have no real answer either to how it came about that half a million German prisoners were wired into camps beside the Rhine for months at the end of the war with no shelter, precious little food, no blankets and no latrines. The official registered death rate in three months was four percent. Was this mass murder too, or the exigency of war?

I invited Schulze-Kossens to our annual regimental dinner and to the Cavalry Memorial Parade in Hyde Park. He came and was locked up at Heathrow until showing his invitation card. On that visit he and his wife met many of his old adversaries in Greece; no one disliked them and they came afterwards to stay for a few days in Devon.

I frequently dream, and could write at length, on the atrocities committed by every nationality and government over those six years of conflict: of the men taken at Stalingrad and imprisoned in the Soviet Union for the rest of their wretched lives; of the massacres of whole populations of occupied villages in France and Czechoslovakia; of the murder of German POWs as they stepped off a plane at Comiso in Sicily; of the torture of German officers in Yugoslav jails after the end of the war, and of the 'repatriation' of the Cossack Regiments into the bloody hands of Stalin. And I am haunted still by the SS officer I saw shot by the Americans after he had tried to show them how the bazooka worked. 'Walk . . . walk . . . run . . .' All these rank highly in any measure of beastliness, except perhaps that of scale, with even the holocaust. We must never forget that the capacity for cruelty – personal and institutionally imposed cruelty – knows no bounds or boundaries. But we must not forget either the Yugoslavs who risked their lives to give us bread on the train on the way from Greece to Germany; the Russian people who gazed with pity on the shackled ranks of Germans as they were paraded through Moscow; the opposition in Germany itself which succeeded in rescuing and hiding Jews: limitless cruelty balanced by courageous compassion. History, if it is to be anything, must be impartial in its reporting and in its judgements.

I have written in this little book of my experiences as a POW and of the largely 'correct' treatment I and the others received there. I have written, too, of the fact that without Red Cross parcels we would have starved, as they starved in concentration camps and as the Russian prisoners starved just a few kilometres away. In contrast, it is interesting to note that the post-war official German commission of enquiry into the treatment of their POWs noted that: 'German prisoners-of-war in England were well-treated, well fed and well housed'. It makes the point that often the daily menus contained a higher calorific value than the rations available to the civilian population. So too it was in the United States and in Canada.

In England, 'trusty' POWs became commonplace. Some 800 married English girls after the war and stayed here. One such was Werner Rang who became a police constable on Sark and ran the souvenir shop; another, Bert Trautmann, kept heroic goal for Manchester City in the 1956 Cup Final. Perhaps the most bemused was the Feldwebel who was given a shot-gun by the farmer who employed him so that he might help keep down the rabbits. No German escaped successfully from a camp in the United Kingdom although Luftwaffe pilots Wappler and Schnabel slipped away from a camp near Penrith and helped themselves to an RAF trainer aircraft. They ran out of fuel and landed at Yarmouth trying to pass themselves off as Dutch. There they were recaptured.

It seems that British prisoners-of-war were psychologically better equipped to cope with captivity than German. Comradeship and humour were our weapons against hunger, cold and deprivation. The Germans, who suffered little apart from loss of liberty, found the ties that bound them together a little looser and the need for a formal and imposed discipline all the more necessary. Political mistrust was a factor which led first to discord and then to the camp 'trials' of those found wanting. There were traitors in most camps, eager to report on their comrades in return for favoured treatment after the war. This situation led to paranoia and sometimes to murder. One U-Boat sailor had given the British so much information on the plans for submarine deployment that, when his room-mates somehow found out, they hanged him in the wash-room. Seven young men, all aged under twenty-three, were found guilty of his murder and executed. Their defence was that as the traitor had caused innumerable deaths among thir fellows in the U-Boat fleet, he deserved to die. It is difficult to condemn, morally, such a judgement.

Other camp trials were not quite so final. Lieutenant Bernhardt Brandt was found guilty by his fellow prisoners of failing to sink his submarine before it was captured by the British, thus surrendering a number of secrets, and was remanded for proper trial after the war. The British newspapers of the time were full of photographs of the boat lying in Barrow docks, and Brandt pleaded with his fellow prisoners to be allowed to escape, make his way to Barrow and repair his omission. As in Warburg it was not all that difficult to get beyond the wire, and he made it to Barrow, only to be shot by an alert dockyard sentry after failing to stop when challenged. His funeral was attended by those who had tried him.

In Yugoslav jails many Germans alleged that they were tortured by their captors into collaboration of the most infamous kind. When the inmates of the Werchetz Camp were released to Germany after the war, the collaborators were repatriated alongside them and were tried in German courts. On the whole the sentences were light: Major Tallarek, found guilty of both beating and hanging fellow inmates, pleaded that he was so tortured by the Yugoslavs that he had no choice; he was sentenced to eighteen months' hard labour. Lieutenant Wilde, a Panzer-Grenadier, alleged that he was tied to a stake for ten days and starved before he agreed to torture his comrades; he got four years.

In POW camps for the British in Germany, the spectre of a camp traitor arose very rarely, and then usually as the result of rather clumsy Teutonic efforts to introduce an English-speaking German into our midst. Without an inborn grasp of English social nuances, such a cuckoo in the nest stood no hope and was laughed out of court.

In Warburg VI B we had, or nearly had, the real thing. A delightful officer whose nerve cracked under the strain of incarceration made it known that he had decided to apply to the Commandant to join the Wehrmacht in order to fight against the Russians. We saved his neck by telling the Commandant that he had gone temporarily nuts. The Commandant agreed.

Index